# GARFIELD'S
## GUIDE TO
# EVERYTHING

# GARFIELD'S GUIDE TO EVERYTHING

### CREATED BY
## JIM DAVIS

### WRITTEN BY
## MARK ACEY AND SCOTT NICKEL

## Ballantine Books • New York

A Ballantine Book
Published by The Random House Publishing Group
Copyright © 2004 by PAWS, Inc. All Rights Reserved.

Published in the United States by Ballantine Books, an imprint of The Random House Publishing Group, a division of Random House, Inc., New York, and simultaneously in Canada by Random House of Canada Limited, Toronto.

Ballantine and colophon are registered trademarks of Random House, Inc.

"GARFIELD" and the GARFIELD characters are registered and unregistered trademarks of PAWS, Inc.

www.ballantinebooks.com

Library of Congress Control Number: 2004095039

ISBN  0-345-46461-3

Manufactured in the United States of America

9  8  7

First Edition: November 2004

# CREDITS

EDITORS AND WRITERS
**MARK ACEY AND SCOTT NICKEL**

ART DIRECTOR
**BETSY KNOTTS**

DESIGNER
**KENNY GOETZINGER**

ILLUSTRATORS
**GARY BARKER, LORI BARKER,
LARRY FENTZ, MIKE FENTZ,
BRETT KOTH, LYNETTE NUDING,
ERIC REAVES**

PRODUCTION ARTIST
**LINDA DUELL**

# CONTENTS



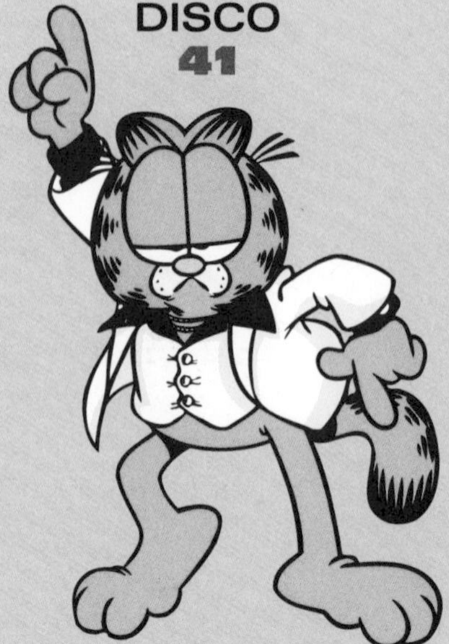

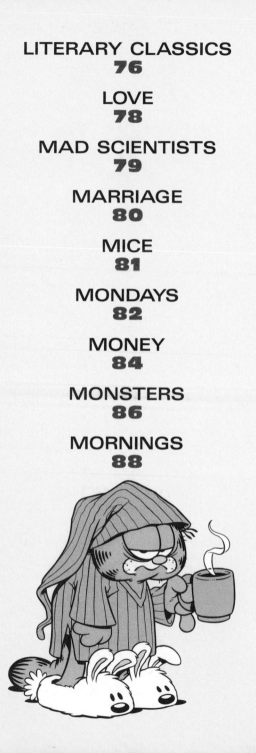

# INTRODUCTION

EVERYONE'S ENTITLED TO MY OPINION

This book contains everything you ever wanted to know about everything (but were too lazy to ask). Okay, so it's actually just my not-so-humble opinions about everything. But I *am* a portly pundit who possesses the gift of gab as well as the gift of flab. And now that I've waddled this earth for more than a quarter century, like most geezers, I feel qualified—even compelled—to inflict my views on everyone.

Thus, I've compiled this cockeyed guide, wherein I weigh in on such matters as mad scientists, mailmen, marriage, messiness, mice, Mondays, money, monsters, mornings, movies, mullets—and that's just the "m's."

I offer interesting info and snide asides on everything from aliens to zits: wacky, tacky, urbane, inane . . . it's all here, expressed in all my grandiose Garfieldian glory.

So, let me be your guide, and enjoy the ride. My words, and welcome to them . . .

# GARFIELD ON ALIENS

**S**trange creatures traveling great distances . . . threatening to invade our homes. Yikes! Sounds like in-laws. But aliens are much scarier. They look like bugs, or lizards, or even worse, like Michael Jackson!

People think they want to conquer our planet. Maybe they're only coming to Earth for the food. I've seen pictures of Mars. It's all rocks and desert. There's not a single waffle house on the whole planet. And there's definitely no drive-thru. Who can blame them for wanting to leave? Maybe it's worth traveling a few thousand light-years for some good chili fries.

YOU EARTHLINGS ARE STRANGE CREATURES. WHAT IS YOUR POWER SOURCE? ATOMIC? SOLAR? BATTERIES?

CAFFEINE

LOG DATE: 2254. CAPTAIN GARFIELD WANDERS THROUGH THE GALAXY

JPM DAVPS 9-27

SEARCHING FOR NEW AND WEIRD LIFE FORMS

GOOD MORNING, GARFIELD

SHORT TRIP

# GARFIELD
## ON
# ART

**W**hen it comes to art, I like the classics: Michelangelo, da Vinci, Rembrandt, and anything on black velvet. I enjoy some of the impressionists, too. Especially that Rich Little guy. But I can't say that I'm a big fan of modern art. Call me an uncultured slob, but I just don't get most of this new stuff.

Take cubism, for example. People with three eyes and six legs and upside-down noses? Who's the blockhead who thought up this goofy style? Then there's abstract expressionism. If this is art then I'm president of Weight Watchers. I think Odie could create better paintings with his tongue. And don't get me started on pop art. A giant soup can? You don't need to go to a museum to see that; just go to Wal-Mart.

Actually, the only modern art I care for is surrealism. Now that's wild stuff. I don't know much about Salvador Dali, but based on his paintings, I bet he was a blast to party with!

# GARFIELD ON ASTROLOGY

**W**hat's my sign? How about "wide load"? Or maybe "will work for donuts."

Actually, my astrological sign is Gemini, the sign of the twins. No wonder I like food so much . . . I'm eating for two.

The roots of the astrology that we know today date all the way back to ancient Mesopotamia (2300 BC). I think it all started at a Mesopotamian singles bar when the pickup line "Hey, baby, what's your sign?" was first uttered.

Modern sun sign astrology (the "Zodiac") came into vogue in the latter part of the twentieth century. This "science" uses a complicated system of planets, constellations, and elements to predict your future. I think a Magic 8-ball is simpler and just as effective.

But if you want to believe that when the Moon is in the seventh house and Jupiter aligns with Mars it's a good day to buy a lottery ticket or start a new relationship, far be it from me to rain on your cosmic parade.

I may be a little skeptical of horoscopes . . . but they can be fun. What do the stars say about you? Let's find out . . .

**MAY 21 ✴ JUNE 20**

**Geminis believe in half the work and twice the fun!**

**Virgo**

> AUG 23 * SEPT 22 <

Industrious and meticulous,
Virgos always do a good job...
and look good doing it.

**Taurus**

> APRIL 20 * MAY 20 <

Straightforward, Taurus
always gives two choices:
take it or leave it.

**Scorpio**

> OCT 23 * NOV 21 <

Scorpios can resist temptation,
but they'd rather not.

**Aries**

> MARCH 21 * APRIL 19 <

Aries never holds a grudge.
They get even right away.

**Capricorn**

> DEC 22 * JAN 19 <

Capricorns are ambitious.
But not till noon.

**Pisces**

> FEB 19 * MARCH 20 <

Easygoing, Pisces will join a gym
when they put in a dessert bar.

**Aquarius**

> JAN 20 * FEB 18 <

Aquarians fear little in life...
except maybe running out of beverages.

**Cancer**

> JUNE 21 * JULY 22 <

Cancers prefer the domestic joys...
family, security, and
a well-stocked refrigerator.

**Leo**

> JULY 23 * AUG 22 <

Leos are brave and loyal, kind and caring.
Their generosity is exceeded only by the
size of their credit-card bills.

**Sagittarius**

> NOV 22 * DEC 21 <

Expressive and sincere (whether
they mean it or not), Sagittarians have
a voracious appetite for life.

**Libra**

> SEPT 23 * OCT 22 <

Fiercely independent,
Libras hate rules...
especially limits on dessert.

**E**veryone dreads getting on the bathroom scale and checking their weight. But for me it's even worse. I have a talking scale that insists on taking jabs at my flab. Over the years it's called me "Lard Ball," "Flabbo," "Tubby," "Blubber Bottom," and "Your Chubbiness." But I've gotten even with my electronic nemesis. I've bashed it, smashed it, walked on it with golf shoes, and even plopped a piano on it.

And while this annoying appliance with the rude attitude may always have the last word, I have the last laugh. Because no matter how witty the scale is, it can't win. It still winds up with a fat cat standing on its face.

YOU JUST GAVE BIRTH TO ANOTHER CHIN!

# GARFIELD ON BODY PIERCING

I don't get it. People used to avoid sticking sharp metal things into their noses, eyebrows, and tongues. Now they can't wait to turn themselves into human pincushions.

Body piercing isn't just unattractive; it's inconvenient, too. Going through an airport metal detector could take hours. And just imagine how gross (and painful) a nose ring gets when you have a head cold. But that's not the worst of it. Ever try eating with a tongue stud? Or grooming yourself? Ouch!

The only body piercing that makes sense is a ring in your navel. At least you could attach your keys to it so you'd never lose them.

What's next for this freaky fad?

Will teenagers resort to piercing internal organs?

APPENDIX

LUNGS

COOOOL

# GARFIELD ON BOWLING

**B**owling is right down my alley. I like it because there's a lot of time to spare. And I use that time, of course, to eat. After I punish some pins, I maim a pizza. Sure, I like launching that ball down the lane; but, ultimately, I'm not all that interested in going for "turkeys" and 10-7 splits. I'd rather go to the snack bar for turkey melts and banana splits!

I also dig the style . . . those hipster shirts and shoes. I am one cool alley cat. I'd rather look great than bowl great. My game is in the gutter, but my garb is on the mark!

Bowling is for the average guy (and my average is my business). In fact, it's big fat hairy fun for everyone! You don't have to be buff or bulked-up on steroids. Forget "hard-body" athletes: my "roll" model is "*wide*-body" Fred Flintstone!

YOU ONLY DATE ATHLETIC TYPES?

JPM DAVPS 11-22

WELL, MARY, I HAVE GOOD NEWS...

© 2002 PAWS, INC. All Rights Reserved.

I'M WEARING BOWLING SHOES!

CLICK

GUTTER BALL

# GARFIELD ON CAMPING

As far as I'm concerned, there's nothing great about the "great outdoors." There's no pizza delivery, you never know where Bigfoot might turn up, and those battery-operated TVs get lousy reception.

Then there are the disgusting bugs. They buzz, they bite, they slink, they slither. They're more annoying than a herd of insurance salesmen.

And who needs a campfire? I've got a microwave at home that'll toast a dozen marshmallows—in twenty seconds, no less.

You can keep your campouts. My idea of "roughing it" is a hotel with no room service.

THE ONLY MOOSE I LIKE IS CHOCOLATE!

WHAT DO YOU THINK OF MY NEW TENT, GARFIELD? I GOT IT ON SALE

GOOSH

SUCH A DEAL

JIM DAVIS 9-19

# GARFIELD
## ON
# CATS

CATS RULE!

**C**ats are regal. The ancient Egyptians worshipped us (obviously an advanced civilization). The pharaohs even had us mummified so we could sack out with them for "the big sleep." (Luckily, we have *nine* lives.) And a recent study found a cat buried alongside a 9,500-year-old human grave on the island of Cyprus. Tells me my noble ancestors held a (well-deserved) place of honor even way back then.

What can I say? To know us is to revere us. True in the past and will be long into the future. Our (ahem) "owners" adore us, so much so that they're putty in our paws. They make the rules; we break the rules. It's a great relationship.

## REASONS TO OWN A CAT INSTEAD OF A DOG

- No need to drool-proof your home
- Cat won't drag you out into blizzard just to piddle on a tree
- Nothing spooks a burglar like stepping on a cat
- Dog breath actually killed a guy in Cincinnati
- Cat has absolutely no romantic interest in your leg

Yes, cats are your best pet bet. Nothing's cozier than a lap full of cat. We're the most fun on four paws! Dogs schmogs. There's no comparison. Cats nap; dogs yap. Cats are clean; dogs, obscene. (Drinking from the toilet? 'Nuff said.) And cats are smart, whereas dogs are actually aliens from a very dumb planet. (That's my theory, and I'm sticking to it.)

But I don't need to put down dogs (though it's always fun) to build up cats. The pharaohs aren't spending eternity with Fido. Case closed.

Cats think / Dogs stink

GARFIELD'S GUIDE TO **EVERYTHING**

**F**orget chestnuts . . . I prefer corn dogs roasting on an open fire. Christmas is my favorite time of year. After all, it features three of the things I love most: food, presents, and more food.

Then there are the special holiday traditions . . . like Jon's annual decorating disasters (he's spent five of the last six Christmas Eves in the ER) and Christmas on the farm (that's when Jon's dad wears his dress overalls).

And who can forget the charming TV shows that celebrate the season? Classics like "Hairy Larry, the Spider Who Saved Christmas" and "Stewey, the Anal-Retentive Elf."

It sometimes seems that Christmas has become too commercial, but I know that the season really is bigger than the biggest package under the tree. I've said it before, and I'll say it again, "Christmas. It's not the giving. It's not the getting. It's the loving."

YOU GOTTA WISH BIG TO GET BIG!

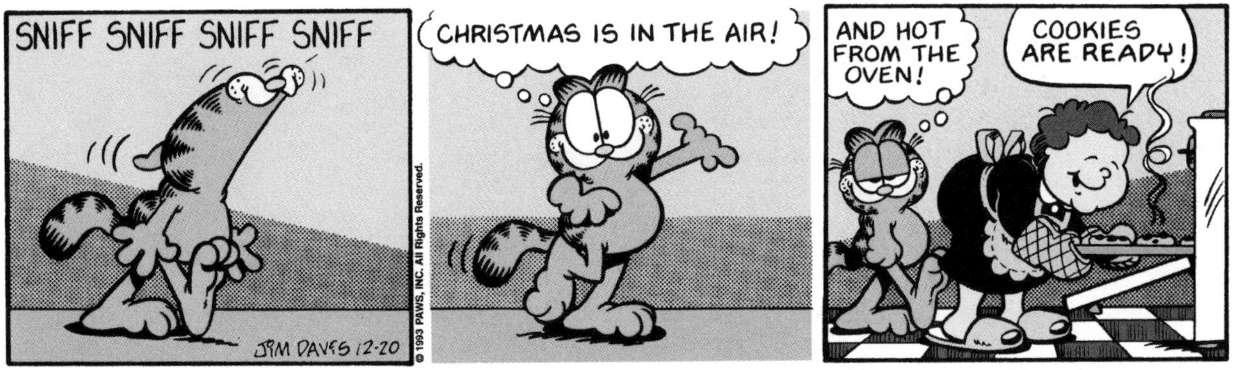
SNIFF SNIFF SNIFF SNIFF
JIM DAVIS 12-20
© 1993 PAWS, INC. All Rights Reserved.
CHRISTMAS IS IN THE AIR!
AND HOT FROM THE OVEN!
COOKIES ARE READY!

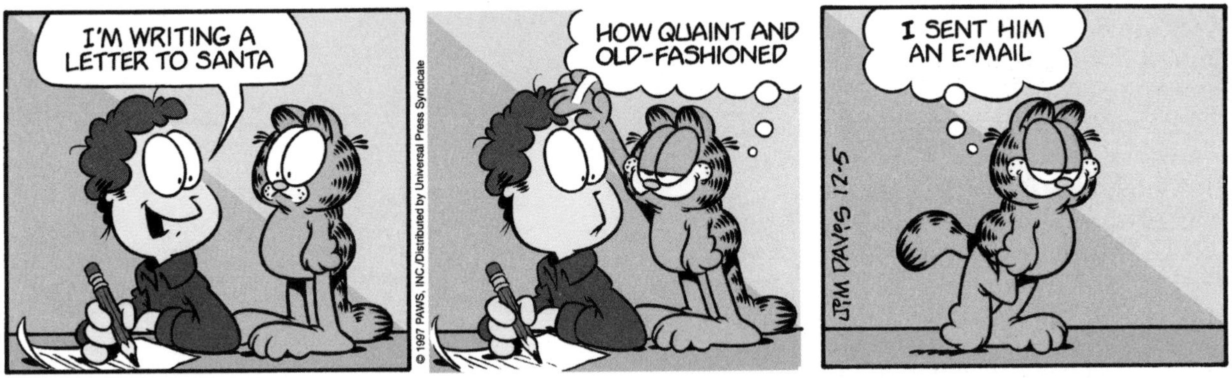
I'M WRITING A LETTER TO SANTA
© 1997 PAWS, INC./Distributed by Universal Press Syndicate
HOW QUAINT AND OLD-FASHIONED
JIM DAVIS 12-5
I SENT HIM AN E-MAIL

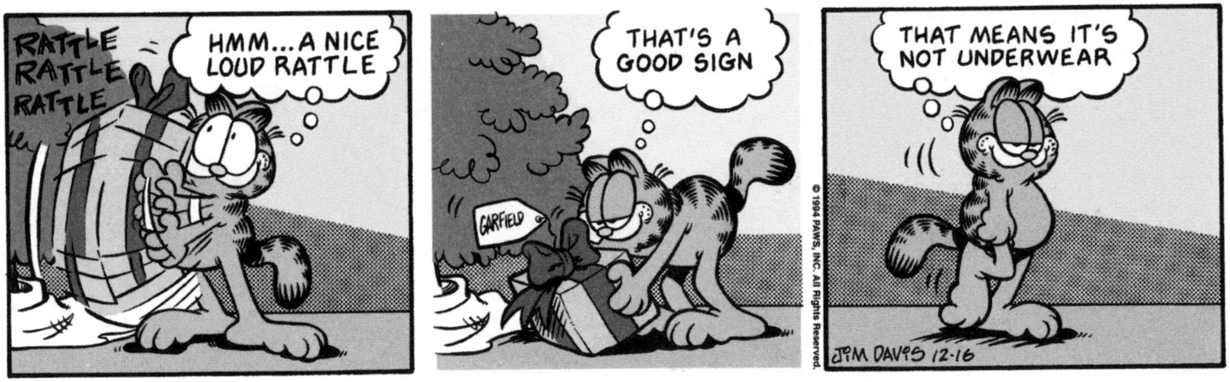
RATTLE RATTLE RATTLE
HMM... A NICE LOUD RATTLE
THAT'S A GOOD SIGN
GARFIELD
© 1994 PAWS, INC. All Rights Reserved.
THAT MEANS IT'S NOT UNDERWEAR
JIM DAVIS 12-16

# GARFIELD ON CLOWNS

**S**ome people are creeped out by clowns; I just find them annoying—always with the horn-honking and the pies in the face. (Pies should be eaten, not thrown!) And thirty clowns trying to wedge themselves into a Volkswagen . . . what's up with that?

All of which is ironic because not only do I live with a clown (Have you seen Jon's wacky wardrobe?), but I was once actually a clown myself! Odie and I ran away from home and joined the circus, where I was forced to work as a clown named "Rotundo." (The indignity!)

But I do like Binky the Clown's TV show. Sure he's OBNOXIOUSLY LOUD (compared to Binky, Krakatoa was a good burp)! But I'll take a loud clown over a dumb mime any day.

**Panel 1:** LADIEEES AND GENTLEMEN! MY ASSISTANT!... ROTUNDO THE CLOWN! / "ROTUNDO"? 9-19

**Panel 2:** ROTUNDO WILL NOW TAKE A PIE IN THE FACE! / SPLUT

**Panel 3:** FROM MY ASSISTANT, DUMMY THE CLOWN! / HE LOOKS VAGUELY FAMILIAR

# Clown Pickup Lines

LET'S GO SOMEWHERE QUIET. THIS PLACE IS A CIRCUS!

DID YOU FIND MY LOST DIAMOND-ENCRUSTED GOLD SLAPSTICK?

ARE YOU KIDDING? OF COURSE I KNOW BOZO!

WHAT A COINKYDINK! THAT'S THE SAME SHADE OF LIPSTICK I WEAR!

A GIRL LIKE YOU COULD REALLY TOOT MY HORN!

Java, joe, cappuccino, espresso . . . it's all coffee, and it's all good. A cup by any other name would taste as great. But here's the thing: this wondrous elixir of life, this cornerstone of civilization—it's gotta be strong. I mean, Hercules strong. In fact, I think he used to down a pot before he bench-pressed an elephant to get in shape.

Decaf? Make me laugh. That stuff's for wimps and wannabees. I'm a caffeine fiend . . . born to be wired! I'm always up for a cup! Especially in the mornings . . . it's the only way to start my day. My eyelids go up when the coffee goes down. Ten or twelve cups, and I can deal with the daily grind.

Coffee. Just brew it.

**Coffee:
Mother Nature's
jumper cables!**

**Taste the bean.
Feel the bean.
Be the bean.**

**Take life
one cup
at a time.**

AND DON'T FORGET TO STOP AND SMELL THE REFILLS ALONG THE WAY...

BEAN ME!

WHAM!

SOMETHING TELLS ME THIS ISN'T YOUR FIRST CUP TODAY

# GARFIELD ON COMPUTERS

Basically, I'm a low-tech tabby. My interest (and energy) doesn't extend much beyond the TV remote control. (I wish they'd invent a remote for *everything*.)

When it comes to computers, I'm ambivalent: They leave me both dazzled and frazzled! I can order pizza online and e-mail my Christmas wish list to Santa; you gotta love that. But computers are always crashing, spying on you, spreading viruses, and generally driving you buggy! Besides, I prefer not to mess with a mouse of any kind.

Sure, I have my own Web site (doesn't everyone?). But as far as I'm concerned, you take the Pentium chips; I'll take the potato chips. (Then I'll take a nap.) I'll get with the program when they come out with a computer that will fix me dinner.

In short, I think I'd rather whack 'em than hack 'em!

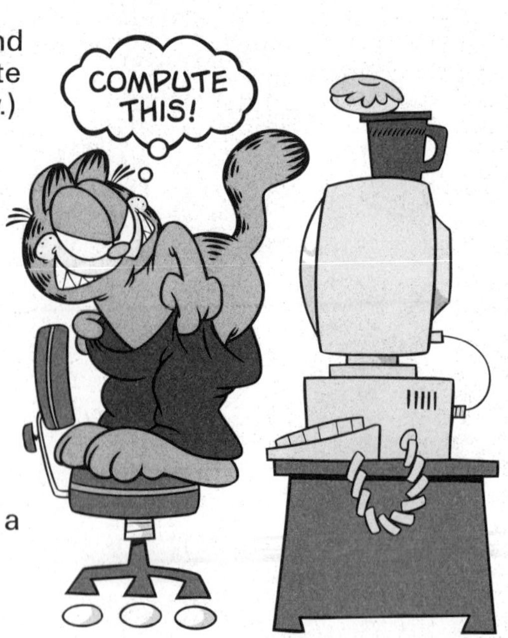
COMPUTE THIS!

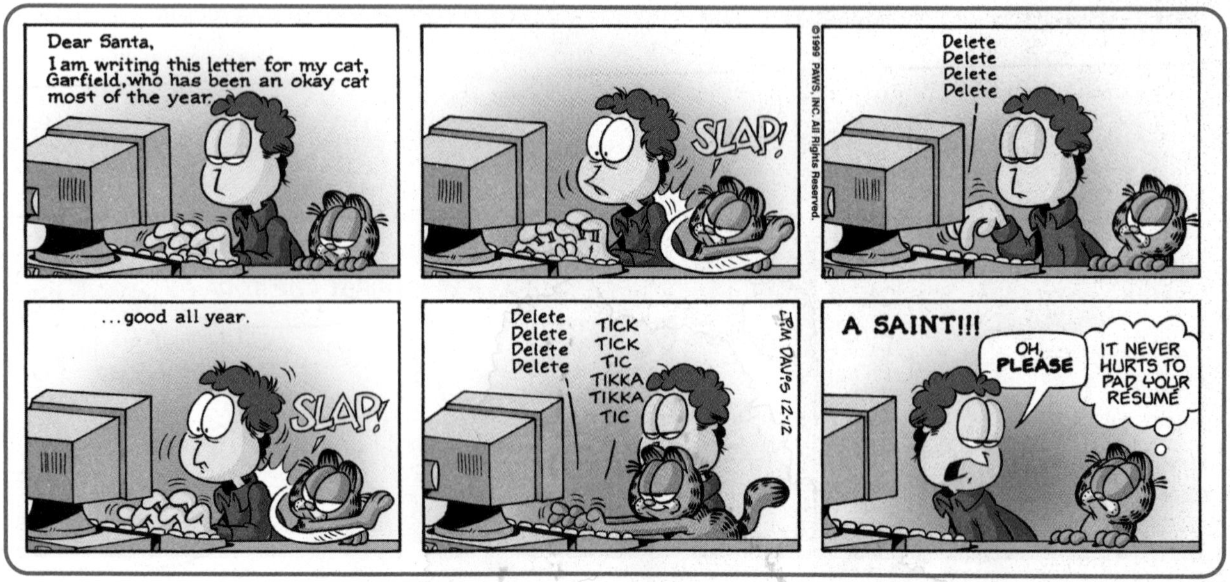
Dear Santa,
I am writing this letter for my cat, Garfield, who has been an okay cat most of the year.
SLAP!
©1999 PAWS, INC. All Rights Reserved.
Delete Delete Delete Delete
...good all year.
SLAP!
Delete Delete Delete Delete
TICK TICK TIC TIKKA TIKKA TIC
JIM DAVIS 12-12
A SAINT!!!
OH, PLEASE
IT NEVER HURTS TO PAD YOUR RESUMÉ

I SURF, THEREFORE
I WIPE OUT.

SORRY, I DON'T DO WINDOWS.

I LOVE MY COMPUTER, BUT
MY COMPUTER HATES ME.

I'VE GOT A HUNDRED
GIGABYTES OF DISK SPACE, AND
SIX PHONE NUMBERS ON IT.

HAVE YOU BOOTED
YOUR COMPUTER
TODAY?

I LOVE MY COMPUTER. IT
MAKES A GREAT PAPERWEIGHT.

HELP! I'M DOWNLOADING
AND I CAN'T GET UP!

**A** brightly lit place fully stocked with every known form of snack, open all the time. You may call it a convenience store. I call it heaven.

Got a craving for a foot-long hoagie at midnight? No problem! Hungry for spicy pork rinds and a microwaveable burrito at 3 a.m.? Got ya covered. And what about those slushies? Icy nectar of the gods. (Just beware of brain freeze!)

It's true that convenience stores are usually staffed by scary-looking ex-cons hopped up on coffee and Twinkies, and some of the "customers" who wander in during the wee hours might be a little strange (can you say serial killer?), but that's a small price to pay for a junk-food connection that can feed your need 24/7.

# GARFIELD
## ON
## COUNTRY MUSIC

**W**hat happens when your wife leaves you, your dog runs away, and your pickup truck dies? If you're a normal person, you go into therapy. If you're from Texas, you write a country song about it.

Country music speaks to the folks who work hard, play hard, and dress funny (what's up with those pointy boots and giant cowboy hats?). And it's as American as mom, apple pie, and trailer parks.

I might even write a few songs myself. How about "Looking for Lunch (in All the Wrong Places)," "Odie from Muskogee," "Mama, Don't Let Your Kittens Grow Up to Be Professional Wrestlers," or maybe "I Burp as Much in Texas as I Did in Tennessee." Yee-haw!

...LIPSTICK ON YOUR FLEA COLLAR, CHEATIN' ON YOUR MIND...

# GARFIELD ON DATING

WILL WORK FOR DATE

The dating scene is never easy, but it's especially hard for my hapless owner, Jon. When he's not being turned down, he's hooking up with the world's weirdest women. Let's see . . . there was Kimmy, who was raised by wolves; Loretta Gnish, who had a third nostril; Big Bertha, who made the circus fat lady seem petite; and of course, who could forget Cindy Krovitz, *Barbershop Digest* cover model? (She had a great handlebar mustache!)

When it comes to dating disasters, Jon's had them all. Once he accidentally shaved half his head, ripped his jacket on the car door, set his tie on fire, and accidentally flushed his contacts down the toilet—all on the same date! Then there was the time his date fell asleep listening to his farm stories and almost drowned in her soup.

But hope springs ever eternal for this clueless Casanova. And as long as he can dial a phone, he'll keep asking women out. Who knows? Maybe someday Jon will get lucky. Yeah . . . and maybe someday Ralph Nader will become president.

THAT'S IT, GARFIELD. I'VE ASKED EVERY GIRL ON THIS BEACH OUT

AND THEY ALL SAID NO

EVEN THE ONE WITH THE HAIRY BACK?

EVEN THE ONE WITH THE HAIRY BACK!

# JON'S SCARIEST DATES

Annie Axelrod, Harley mechanic

Gertie, Greta, and Bob, Siamese Triplets

Suki the Sumo Belly Dancer

Garfield

# GARFIELD ON DICTIONARIES

**A**ccording to the dictionary, the word "dictionary" means "a reference book containing words usually alphabetically arranged along with their forms, pronunciations, functions, etymologies, meanings, and syntactical and idiomatic uses." Say what? That makes dictionaries sound boring and "off-putting"—like the word "off-putting."

According to me, dictionaries are a place where words live. Big, gargantuan words and little, lilliputian words; dull, stodgy words and snazzy, jazzy words. They all live together in perfect alphabetical harmony. Me, I like the weird, wacky, whimsical ones (*gizzard*, *goiter*, *bloomers*, *bagpipes*). And, *bodacious*, *cattylicious*, *funky furball* that I am, I love to sling the slang! Word up!

I also like to give more mundane words my own daffy definitions. See, I even wrote 'em down, so you don't have to look 'em up.

# DaFfy DeFiNItiOns

**alarm clock**: A device for waking people who don't have kids or pets.

**Arbuckle**: From the Latin *arbuculus*, "wiener-chested"; a geek; a nerd; a geeky nerd; you get the picture.

**bed**: Furniture piece designed for that most exciting of all activities—sleep.

**bird**: A feathered flying cat snack.

**brother**: A common household pest; synonymous with "bother."

**calories**: The best-tasting bits of any food. Take thousands, they're small.

BIRD

**cat**: A highly intelligent and attractive animal of the feline persuasion; nature's most perfect pet.

**chocolate**: A sweet, highly fattening substance; one of the four basic food groups.

**Christmas**: December holiday that promotes the spirit of getting; also has some religious significance.

**claw**: A cat's best friend; a drape's worst nightmare.

**diet**: An eating program that removes excess pounds and your will to live.

**dog**: A brainless, four-legged flea magnet whose breath could stun a moose.

**dream**: A fantasy, like no-cal lasagna, or a woman who thinks Jon is cool.

**eat**: What one does between naps.

**exercise**: Any completely unnecessary physical activity, such as jogging, or rolling over.

**fat**: Overweight; obese; Santa-waisted; in other words, just right.

**french fries**: Slivers of potato cooked in hot oil; best when eaten, or stuck in your nose.

**Halloween**: Ancient Celtic celebration of the dead, which has evolved quite nicely into an excuse to eat candy until you explode.

**homework**: Cruel and unusual punishment, best suffered in front of the TV.

**kitten**: A small, cuddly animal used to trick people into buying cats.

**lasagna**: Nature's most perfect food.

**lazy**: Indolent, slothful; in extreme cases, comatose.

KITTEN

**mailman**: One who delivers the mail; see also scratching post.

**morning**: The bad end to a good night; would be much better if it started later.

**mouse**: Furry, germ-infested, cheese-licking rodent. This is suitable cat cuisine? I don't think so.

**Nermal**: The world's cutest kitten, soon to become extinct.

**Odie**: A type of dog, or fungus; it's hard to tell.

**parent**: An adult keeper of children; not easily understood, but at least they provide snacks and TV.

**party**: A type of fun assembly guaranteed by the Constitution; see also soiree, wingding, riot.

**pet**: A domestic animal who provides love and companionship in exchange for blind obedience and twelve square meals a day.

ODIE

**pizza**: Delicious tomato and cheese plant that scientists have trained to grow in flat, cardboard boxes. It's true!

**Pooky**: A huggable "beddy" bear who never says a harsh word . . . or anything else.

**school**: An educational institution designed to train your brain, assuming they can find it.

**sister**: An annoying female sibling usually found in the bathroom.

**sleep**: A state of unconsciousness best experienced in large quantities; also, the perfect exercise.

**snoring**: The loud, irritating breathing of a sleeper; easily remedied with a pair of cymbals.

**spider**: Web-spinning, eight-legged insect; generally harmless, especially if bludgeoned with a sledge hammer.

**teacher**: One who instructs; comes in "good," "bad," and "ogre" models.

**telephone**: A communication device permanently attached to an adolescent's ear.

**television**: Device that receives mind-numbing video signals; don't grow up without it.

**tomorrow**: The best time for starting anything unpleasant, like homework or a diet.

**veterinarian**: A doctor who treats animals, whether they like it or not; synonymous with "needles as long as your arm."

GARFIELD'S GUIDE TO EVERYTHING

# GARFIELD ON **DIETS**

**W**ebster's defines it as "a special or limited selection of food and drink, chosen and prescribed to promote health and loss of weight." I call it cruel and unusual punishment.

The list of these gastronomical tortures is seemingly endless: the low-fat diet; the no-fat diet; the Grapefruit diet; the Hollywood 48-Hour Miracle diet; the Cabbage Soup diet; the Sugar Busters diet; the Protein Power diet; Weight Watchers; Atkins; The Zone . . . and on, and on, and on!

I only diet under duress (and only when the vet makes me). And when it comes to cutting back, it's not the hunger pangs that bother me or the hallucinations (ever had a jelly donut try to seduce you?); it's the fact that when I go on a diet, the first thing I lose is my sense of humor.

**I ONLY DIET BETWEEN MEALS.**

**A DIET IS TOO LITTLE OF A GOOD THING.**

**EVERYTHING TASTES GOOD ON A DIET.**

**DIET IS "DIE" WITH A "T."**

# GARFIELD
## ON
# DINERS

**W**hen it comes to restaurants, nothing's finer than a diner. Forget those upscale, chichi eateries; gimme a good ol' greasy spoon any day.

Fine dining, especially, is a pain in the derrière, what with snooty maître d's and all those different forks arranged ever so properly. Besides, I don't *dine*; I strap on the feedbag! And there's no better place to chow down than a diner.

Diners reek with *ambiance*; but there, it'd simply be called *atmosphere*. I particularly like places with a counter and stools, gleaming with Formica and chrome. Add a bottomless mug of coffee served by a gum-cracking waitress, and I'm in hash heaven.

Over the years, Jon and I have had many memorable experiences at Irma's diner. Oh, sure, we've had some unsavory moments—a false eyelash in the french fries, a hoof in my hamburger—but hey, that's all part of the down 'n' dirty charm.

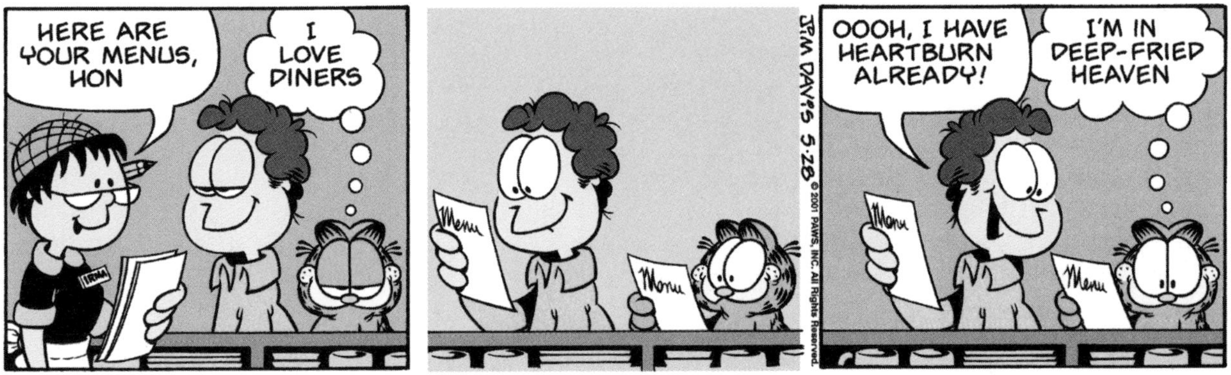
HERE ARE YOUR MENUS, HON
I LOVE DINERS
JIM DAVIS 5-28
© 2001 PAWS, INC. All Rights Reserved.
OOOH, I HAVE HEARTBURN ALREADY!
I'M IN DEEP-FRIED HEAVEN

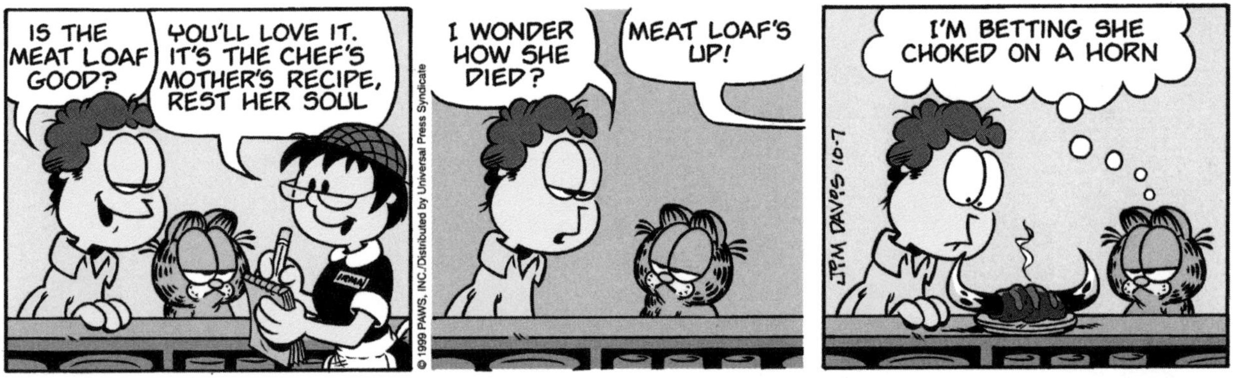
IS THE MEAT LOAF GOOD?
YOU'LL LOVE IT. IT'S THE CHEF'S MOTHER'S RECIPE, REST HER SOUL
© 1999 PAWS, INC./Distributed by Universal Press Syndicate
I WONDER HOW SHE DIED?
MEAT LOAF'S UP!
JIM DAVIS 10-7
I'M BETTING SHE CHOKED ON A HORN

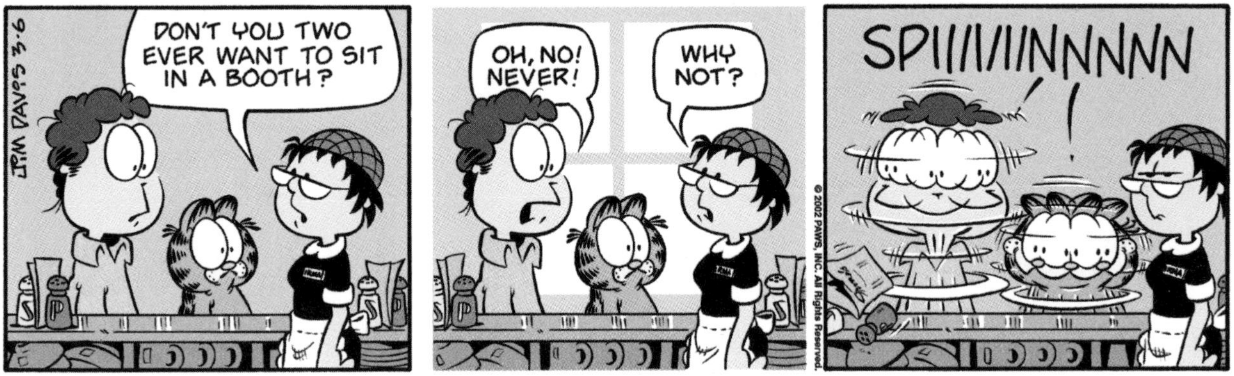
JIM DAVIS 3-6
DON'T YOU TWO EVER WANT TO SIT IN A BOOTH?
OH, NO! NEVER!
WHY NOT?
© 2002 PAWS, INC. All Rights Reserved.
SPIIIIIINNNNN

# GARFIELD
## ON
# DINOSAURS

**W**hat killed off the dinosaurs? Was it a giant comet crashing to Earth, instantly wiping out millions in a single cataclysmic event? Was it the ice age slowly changing the environment and freezing out the giant creatures? Or was it a sedentary lifestyle, together with a steady diet of fatty foods and smoking that ultimately did them in?

I'm no anthropologist, but I have my own theory. I think the dinosaurs became extinct because of Og the caveman. According to cave paintings I've seen, Og was a prehistoric entrepreneur who started the first chain of fast-food caves. The menu? Dino Burgers, Bronto beef ribs, and Broasted Pterodactyls. Talk about a super-sized value meal!

# GARFIELD
## ON
# DISCO

I have a fond place in my hips for disco—after all, I was born during its heyday in the '70s. (And I've been shaking my groove thing ever since!)

**SATURDAY NIGHT FELINE**

By the early '80s they said disco was dead, but this booty-shakin' music refuses to die. So what makes people still want to boogie oogie oogie? It can't be the "meaningful" song lyrics ("That's the way—uh-huh, uh-huh—I like it— uh-huh, uh-huh"), or the "tasteful" fashions (shirts open to the navel, gold medallions, shiny polyester, chunky platform shoes). It must be the beat. That thumpin', groovin', boogyin' beat. It drives perfectly sane people to step out on a dance floor and make complete Arbuckles of themselves. (Have you seen Jon shake it?)

POLYESTER PICTURES PRESENTS SATURDAY NIGHT FELINE   A GARFIELD FILM STARRING GARFIELD AND A BUNCH OF ACTORS YOU NEVER HEARD OF   DIRECTOR OF PHOTOGRAPHY GARFIELD   MUSIC BY GARFIELD EXECUTIVE PRODUCER GARFIELD   SUPREME ALL-KNOWING PRODUCER GARFIELD   WRITTEN BY GARFIELD CHOREOGRAPHED BY GARFIELD   CATERED BY GARFIELD   PRODUCED AND DIRECTED BY TAKE A GUESS A BIG FAT HAIRY PRODUCTION

# GARFIELD
## ON
## DOGS

**W**hat can I say about the canine species? How about life's a bowl of cherries, and dogs are the pits. Or a dog's breath is worse than his bite. Or maybe this: Dogs are the animal by-products in the weenie of life.

Why am I so down on these four-legged flea farms? Maybe it's because they contain 90% of the world's drool supply and the only trick most dogs can do is "play stupid." What positive contribution do these toilet-lappers make to society? Fetching a stick isn't exactly an accomplishment worthy of the Nobel Prize.

As far as I'm concerned, the only good dog is a hot dog.

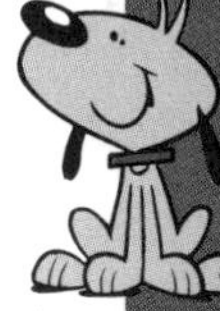

A dog is man's best friend

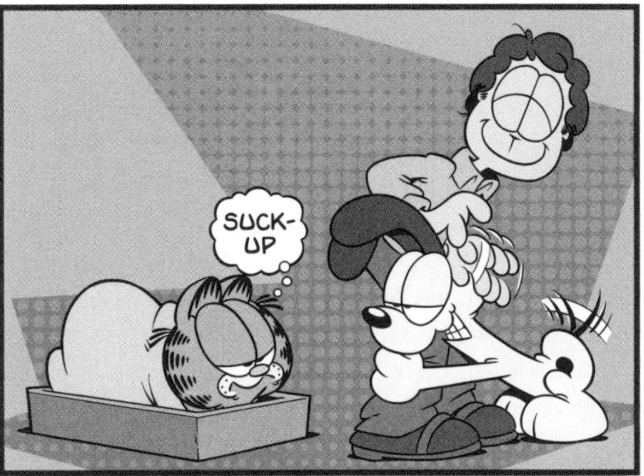
SUCK-UP

Dogs enjoy exercise

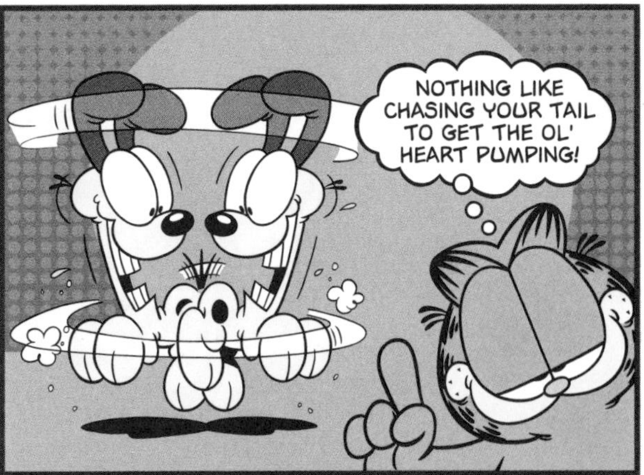
NOTHING LIKE CHASING YOUR TAIL TO GET THE OL' HEART PUMPING!

Dogs make good pets

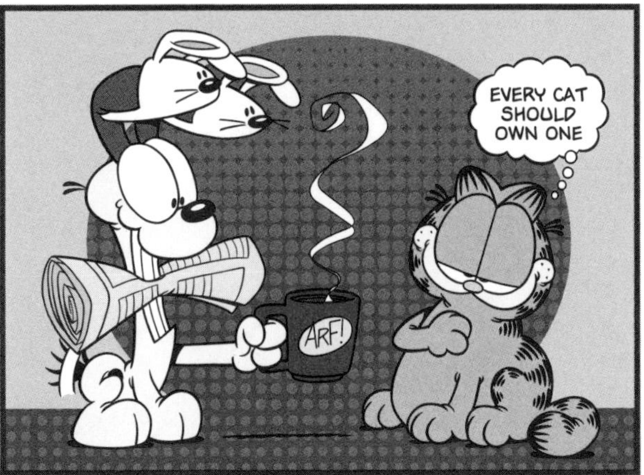
ARF!
EVERY CAT SHOULD OWN ONE

# GARFIELD ON DONUTS

**SLAM DUNK!**

The early bird may get the worm, but the early cat gets the jelly-filled donut. And forget the flowers; I think that in life it's important to take time to stop and smell the donuts (and then, of course, eat them).

When it comes to these sugary confections, I'm an equal-opportunity enjoyer: I love 'em glazed, frosted, chocolate-covered, powdered-sugared, cream-filled, with sprinkles, or just plain.

In my next life I hope I come back as a cop, just so I can hang out in donut shops at two in the morning (and also so I can say things like "Freeze, Slimeball!" . . . but I digress).

And I bet you didn't know that this glorious snack food is actually good for your health. You can get quite a workout dunking a dozen donuts.

I could go on, but I'll leave you with this . . . when it comes to donuts, hole is where the heart is.

YOU NEED TO EAT A MORE BALANCED DIET

BALANCED?

YOU MEAN AS IN MORE THAN ONE KIND OF DONUT?

© 1999 PAWS, INC./Distributed by Universal Press Syndicate

www.garfield.com

JIM DAVIS 7-24

# GARFIELD
## ON
# ECOLOGY

I may be an orange cat, but I'm green at heart. I believe in keeping the Earth green, which is why I gave up salads. Green is a great color for trees, grass, and old food.

I love trees . . . especially with a hammock strung between them. I'm a staunch believer in conserving energy, which is why I nap a lot. In fact, I'm so into ecology, I've got moss growing on my north side. I'm even growing a rain forest in Jon's sock drawer!

But seriously, it's not nice to pollute Mother Nature: So remember . . . a clean planet is a happy planet.

# GARFIELD
## ON
# EDUCATION

**E**ducation: It's all that separates us from the stupid. It's the cure for the common clod. It's the best thing to happen to your head since hair! Hey, this isn't hype; I'm serious. Cool cats know the value of education: Without it, you might as well be a dumb dog, drooling your life away.

We all have brains; some of us just don't use them. Which is a shame, because an unused brain will "Odie-fy": It'll dry out, shrivel up, and chunks of it could eventually fall out of your nose! It's a fate worse than dog breath.

So, if you want to get ahead, you have to use your head and do the bright thing. And that means school. Sure it's work, but it's worth it. You can really profit from the experience: The more you learn, the more you earn.

But education is about more than money. It enriches you in other ways, from the lessons you learn to the friendships you form. Education teaches you how to think (lest your brain shrink) and, ultimately, turns you into a class act!

> AN EDUCATION. DON'T LEAVE SCHOOL WITHOUT IT

DIPLOMA

A OK

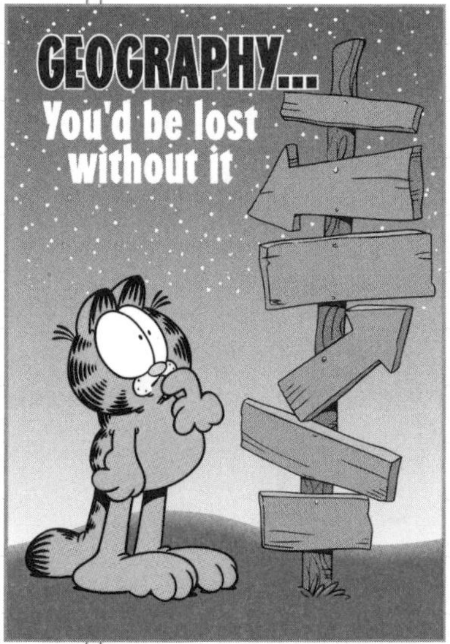
GEOGRAPHY...
You'd be lost without it

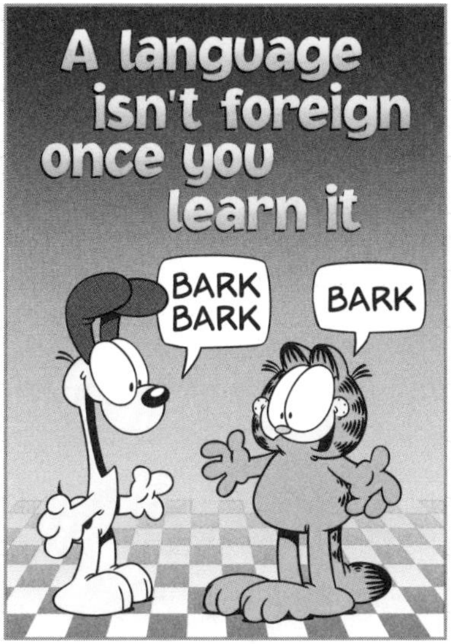
A language isn't foreign once you learn it
BARK BARK
BARK

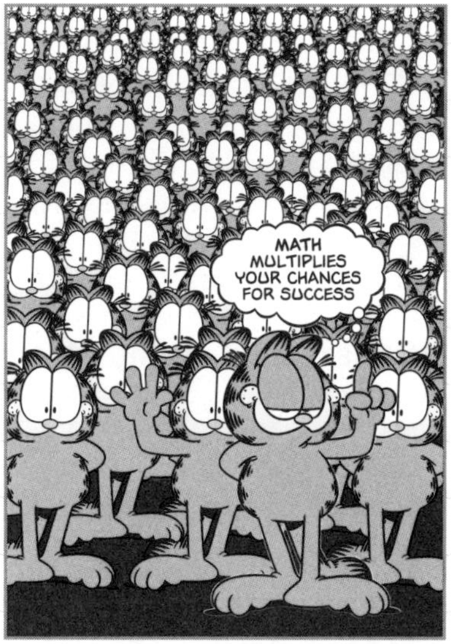
MATH MULTIPLIES YOUR CHANCES FOR SUCCESS

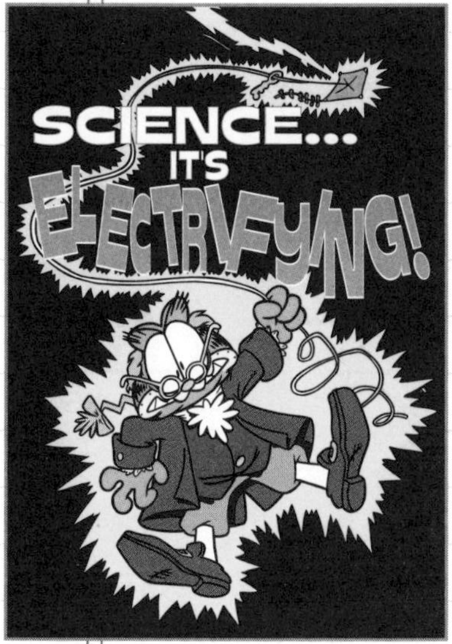
SCIENCE... IT'S ELECTRIFYING!

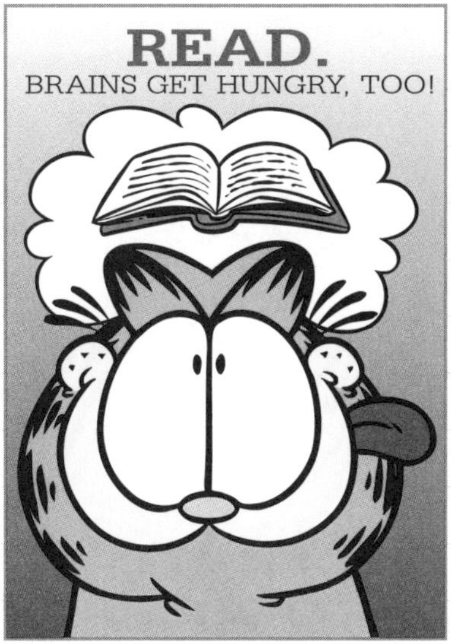
READ.
BRAINS GET HUNGRY, TOO!

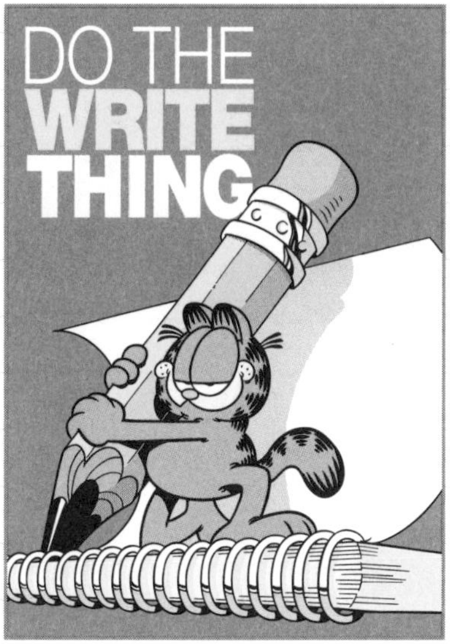
DO THE WRITE THING

**A**t birth, I weighed five pounds six ounces—and four of that was ego. While other kittens said "Meow," I said "Me first." As I've grown, so has my ego (and, of course, my waistline)—so large, in fact, that it's reportedly affected the orbits of neighboring planets. But hey, that's a good thing: A healthy ego is a happy ego.

Obviously, I was destined for greatness. I mean, all I had to do was look in the mirror (and take a bow). No way is Mother Nature gonna waste that kind of charisma on a common mouser. I'm so cool, James Dean could have taken lessons from *me*. I oughta be in pictures—and I was, starring in my own feature film. (Jennifer Love Hewitt couldn't keep her paws off me!)

My secret? I'm in touch with my inner egomaniac at all times. Like I always say, "A little ego goes nowhere." That's why I live large and am always in charge!

I used to be Perfect

I'm Now Even Better!

# GARFIELD
## ON
# EXCUSES

**S**ome people believe in working hard. I, on the other hand, believe in hardly working. Why kill yourself making a living when making excuses is far easier?

That's right. Excuses are your friends. Who needs the stress of showing up on time? When asked why you're late, just say, "I couldn't jump-start my alarm clock," or "I was attacked by a platoon of army ants."

If your room is a mess, simply utter, "I'm allergic to cleanliness," or "Doing chores gives me a rash."

You get the idea. Here are a few more excellent excuses to help you explain why you couldn't, shouldn't, or wouldn't do this, that, or the other!

**WHY I DON'T HAVE MY HOMEWORK...**
I left my brain in my locker.

**WHY I WAS LATE...**
I fell in a puddle of dog drool.

**WHY I WAS ABSENT...**
Two words: alien abduction!

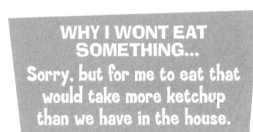

**WHY I CAN'T GO OUT WITH YOU...**
Sorry, but that's my night to floss the dog.

I FORGOT TO REMEMBER!

**WHY I WONT EAT SOMETHING...**
Sorry, but for me to eat that would take more ketchup than we have in the house.

**WHY THIS PLACE IS SUCH A MESS...**
I was frightened at an early age by a vacuum cleaner.

**WHY I'M STILL ON THE PHONE...**
Would you believe the receiver's stuck to my head again?

# GARFIELD
## ON
# EXERCISE

If I were president, I'd ban exercise and conserve our national supply of sweat! Hey, exercise is nothing to lose sweat over. I mean, if we were meant to sweat, we'd have been born with wristbands.

Let's face it—exercise is a pain. If fitness is so healthy, why does it hurt so much? I think people who want to "feel the burn" are either consumed with self-loathing or they're loafing-impaired. Me, I'll take *fatness* over *fitness* any day.

But, personally, I don't even consider myself out of shape. In fact, I have a classic shape. ("Round" is classic, isn't it?) And it's not like I don't get *any* exercise: I just prefer lie-downs to sit-ups. I also do leg-of-lamb lifts, channel surf, and regularly stretch the truth. But as far as I'm concerned, *chewing* is the perfect exercise!

OKAY, CAMPERS, IT'S TIME TO EXERCISE! LET'S START WITH SOME LEG LIFTS... READY, BEGIN!

ANNND **ONE** AND...

CLICK

TWO

© 1989 PAWS, INC. All Rights Reserved.

9-4

JIM DAVIS

I think I'll settle for buns of marshmallow.

An important part of any fitness program is a balanced breakfast.

Exercise is one of my favorite spectator sports!

Working out just isn't working out.

# GARFIELD
## ON
# FARMS

**E**very so often, my dopey owner Jon packs us up and heads to the country to visit his family on their farm. I really enjoy it there . . . about as much as I enjoy going on a diet.

Being a kitty from the city, I think farms are duller than dirt. Oh, sure, there are a few things I like to do on the Arbuckle farm: baste the hogs, harvest the fridge, fertilize Doc Boy's overalls. And I always enjoy "hitting the hay." But my favorite thing to do is leave!

**DON'T YOU GET A LITTLE BORED HERE ON THE FARM, DOC BOY?** **NO WAY!**

**NOW BE QUIET. WE'RE MISSING THE SHOW**

**THERE GOES THE RED SOCK AGAIN!**

**WE COULDN'T AFFORD DOCTORS ON THE FARM**

**WE RELIED ON NATURAL REMEDIES**

**DID YOU KNOW THAT KISSING A CHICKEN CURES COLD SORES?** **GET AWAY FROM ME**

# GARFIELD ON FASHION

**C**lothes make the man. And sometimes they make the man look stupid: Remember Boy George? Liberace? Any guy you've ever seen in a kilt?

But let's not discriminate: Women can be equal fashion disasters. Cher is a Hall of Shamer. Paris Hilton (when she's wearing clothes!) is a walking wardrobe malfunction. And who can forget Bjork's bizarre swan tutu at the Oscars. What *was* she thinking? Sure I'm being catty, but hey, I'm a cat!

And I should know a fashion faux pas when I see it. After all, I live with Jon "Urkel" Arbuckle. A paragon of sartorial splendor he ain't. The Fashion Police have an APB out on some of his outfits.

So what's the "hautest" couture . . . the perfect thing to wear? Personally, I prefer fur—but just for us animals, please. It's classic . . . and classics are always in style. For the rest of you would-be fashionistas, I suggest you wear something in basic orange and black. Hey, it's always worked for me!

## WHAT THE WELL-DRESSED CAT IS WEARING

| TEA LENGTH | OFF THE SHOULDER | MINI | BACKLESS |

I live life in the fat lane because fat is where it's at! Now, obviously, I'm not talking so fat it takes a crane to haul your carcass out of the house. You gotta be able to walk—or at least waddle. But sumo is primo: Those beefy boys are still athletes. And remember the football player William "The Refrigerator" Perry? These guys prove fatsos can be national heroes.

A corpulent couple of my roly-poly role models are King Henry VIII and Orson Welles. Nobody could dispose of a drumstick (or a wife) like His Royal Rotundness. And Orson was an enormous figure in the world of cinema (and cinnamon rolls). Oh, and let's not forget about ol' Saint Nick: Santa just wouldn't be the same without the gut.

I'll take Aunt Bee over Ally McBeal any day. (What *does* Popeye see in Olive Oyl?) And those emaciated fashion models? Those twigs need my help. Hey, who better than me to be a "fatness guru"?

WHEW! I WAS BEGINNING TO THINK I'D NEVER GET FULL. BURP!

# YOU KNOW YOU'RE GETTING **FAT** WHEN...

**SOMEONE TRIES TO CLIMB YOUR NORTH SLOPE**

**NASA ORBITS A SATELLITE AROUND YOU**

**YOU HAVE THIS TREMENDOUS URGE TO GRAZE**

WARNING!

GLUTTON AT LARGE

**YOUR PICTURE IS POSTED IN "ALL-YOU-CAN-EAT" RESTAURANTS**

# GARFIELD
## ON
# FIGURE SKATING

**T**wits in tights prancing around on the ice to classical music. How did this become a sport? Okay, so it's not as boring as ballet, but it's definitely not must-see TV. Maybe if they released a polar bear or a snow leopard into the rink or let the audience try to bean the skaters with snowballs, figure skating might be a little more interesting.

I admit I don't know much about the actual skating moves: double axle, triple lutz, triple toe loop—I can't tell 'em apart. But I do know one move, and it's my favorite. I call it the triple *klutz*. That's when an ice skater falls on his rump three times during a routine.

THESE OUTFITS ARE JUST SCREAMING FOR ACCESSORIES

LIZ IS GOING TO BE SO IMPRESSED, GARFIELD

6-29 JIM DAVIS

© 1989 PAWS, INC. All Rights Reserved.

WATCH OL' JON WORK HIS SKATING MAGIC ON HER!

MY HERO

# GARFIELD ON FISHING

This "sport" combines my two favorite activities: lying motionless for hours and eating. Even if the fish aren't biting, I am. I make sure Jon packs plenty of snacks for our trips. He's not much of a fisherman, but he's hooked some whoppers in his day: a spare tire, an old boot, and, of course, himself.

There are many different types of fishing: freshwater, saltwater, deep-sea. I particularly enjoy indoor freshwater fishing. Never heard of it? It doesn't require bait, hooks, or poles. All you need is a fishbowl, a tasty goldfish, and an easily distracted owner.

**F**ood, glorious food! That's all *I* live for (followed by a long glorious nap). And I mean that from the bottom of my stomach.

Yep, to me, the best things in life are edible. Just the mere thought of a pan of ooey, gooey, chewy, cheesy lasagna sends me into a ravenous rapture! Oh, and a tray of warm chocolate-chip cookies fresh from the oven—be still my beating taste buds!

I'm always in the mood for food: fried food, fast food . . . anything but health food. I crave good quality in great quantities: A full tummy is a happy tummy! Sure, all my food goes to *waist*—but hey, I'd rather be happy than thin.

Lasagna...
nature's perfect food.

One good meal
deserves another.

Too much food
is never enough.

Life is short.
Eat now.

# GARFIELD
## ON
# FRIENDS

The Beatles once sang, "I get by with a little help from my friends." I prefer to get pie with a little help from mine.

We all need friends (and not just the TV show!). Without friends, who would we share our hopes, dreams, (and popcorn) with? While my best friends will always be me, myself, and I, I still enjoy hangin' with my homies, Jon and Odie. Jon keeps my food dish full and the cable bill paid; Odie obeys my every command and makes a great scratching post. What more could a cat ask for?

And while we may have our ups and downs (what buddies don't occasionally bicker?), I wouldn't trade my friends for anything . . . although, I admit, I might be momentarily tempted by a 60" plasma widescreen TV and a lifetime supply of bacon cheeseburgers.

SIGH...I HAVE NO FRIENDS

HEY, PAL!

ZIP

WISHFUL THINKING

JIM DAVIS 11-27

# GARFIELD
## ON
# GANGSTERS

**A**l Capone, Bonnie and Clyde, Don Corleone, Tony Soprano . . . whether fact or fiction, gangsters are fascinating characters. These "goodfellas"—and very bad people—have been romanticized and immortalized, particularly in the movies (and even pizza parlors!).

These robbin' hoods have a strange hold on America's consciousness and a special place in its heart. Is it simply our love of violence? Or is it because gangsters dare to venture outside the law and societal rules? Or maybe that they do it with *style*—swashbuckling pirates in pinstripes? Personally, don't know, don't care: I just want to sit back and enjoy the fireworks.

Of course, I'm too nice to be a *real* gangster. Plus, I'm too messy for organized crime. But I am a wiseguy by nature, possessor of a sharp tongue and a killer wit. So, it's fun to imagine what it would be like to have my own mob. Naturally, I'd be the boss: Just call me "Don Lasagna" (alias: "The Garfather"). Now, I just need some henchmen . . .

# GARFIELD
## ON
# GEEZERS

I used to enjoy making fun of the elderly. I still do, but now that I've been around for over a quarter century (in dog years, I'd be dead!), my humor is occasionally of the self-deprecating variety. But don't get me wrong—I'm not *old* . . . I'm "geezerlicious." I can still shake it . . . I just can't get it to stop!

Fortunately, as you get older, you get wiser (and wider). You learn that the secret to slowing down the aging process is speeding up the lying process. I also recommend eating lots of junk food—you'll need all the preservatives you can get. And I think it's important to age *dis*gracefully. Maturity is overrated: You're only young once, but you can be immature forever!

So, just sit back in your rocking chair, take your teeth out, and enjoy it: Age happens.

I PREFER CHRONOLOGICALLY CHALLENGED

AGE IS A STATE OF MIND

WITH A HEALTHY DOSE OF DENIAL

GARFIELD'S GUIDE TO **EVERYTHING**

YOU KNOW YOU'RE GETTING OLD WHEN

...you put tenderizer on your oatmeal!

WANT ME TO CUT THAT UP FOR YOU?

...you knew Bigfoot when he wore booties!

GOO

...you remember when Baskin-Robbins only had two flavors!

SOME THINGS DO IMPROVE WITH AGE!

...you play connect-the-dots on your liver spots!

HMM...LOOKS LIKE A ONE-EYED, THREE-LEGGED GILA MONSTER PITCHING HORSESHOES

**J**udging from my experiences with Jon over the years, golf is often a four-letter word for stress. ("Golf" spelled backward is "flog." Think about it.) Tee 'em high, let 'em fly . . . start to cry.

When Jon hits the links, the links hit back. (Which is why *my* favorite "links" are sausage.) Jon's handicap is his swing. He did once shoot a 68—on one hole! The

**Take golf one tantrum at a time.**

**Never let 'em see you cheat.**

police arrested him for reckless driving! And the only thing uglier than his game is his garb. "Grip it and rip it" should apply equally to his scorecard and his knickers.

Despite it all, I do my best as his trusted caddy to help him . . . *cheat*. Hey, all's fair in love and golf. If at first you don't succeed . . . change your score when no one's looking! As far as I'm concerned, that's just par for the course.

**Should I use the wedge or the weed-whacker?**

**I'm a scratch golfer in a parallel universe.**

**The perfect partner is anyone worse than I am.**

**A good caddy is always there when you need him.**

# GARFIELD
## ON
# HALLOWEEN

**G**oing door to door demanding candy? Now that's my idea of a holiday! Halloween is one of my favorite times of year. I love carving pumpkins, dressing up, and eating twice my weight in candy corn.

Where did this slightly peculiar holiday come from? Halloween has its origins in Celtic Ireland during the fifth century BC. October 31 was the Celtic New Year, a day in which the disembodied spirits of all those who had died throughout the preceding year would come back in search of living bodies to possess for the next year. Sounds like quite a party, right?

In the 1840s, Halloween came to America. A favorite prank at that time was tipping over outhouses. That's a nice touch, although I've always preferred egging houses.

Today, most people celebrate Halloween by dressing up and going trick-or-treating. I love walking through the neighborhood stocking up on goodies, but I haven't always been dressed for success (thanks to my clueless owner, Jon). Here are a few of my costume catastrophes . . .

GARFIELD'S LEAST FAVORITE HALLOWEEN COSTUMES

Tree

Fire Hydrant

Giant Chew Bone

# GARFIELD
## ON
# HAPPINESS

**M**ost people make finding happiness way too complicated. You don't need to be rich, or handsome, or famous to find bliss. I'm sure somewhere there are poor, ugly, unknown people who are perfectly happy.

There are many roads that lead to happiness. I prefer the one with the most rest stops. As you know, I don't like to work at anything—especially being happy. Give me a soft bed, a big-screen TV, and a few slave dogs to fetch me snacks, and I'm one contented kitty.

## Happiness is sleeping through a Monday

GARFIELD, I WONDER WHAT **TRUE** HAPPINESS REALLY IS...

CLONK

FILL IT UP OR I'LL SHOW YOU WHAT IT AIN'T

JIM DAVIS 6-2 © 2003 PAWS, INC. All Rights Reserved.

# GARFIELD
## ON
# HEAVY METAL

It's loud. It's lewd. It's overblown and offensive. The only thing it's really good for is driving your parents nuts and annoying your neighbors. I can't bring myself to actually listen to this sonic swill (my IQ would have to drop twenty or so points first) but I do like its potential as a weapon of mass distraction.

In fact, the next time my neighbor, Mrs. Feeny, rats me out for eating her flower garden, I'm gonna open the windows, put on a CD of the most obnoxious headbanger band available, and crank it up to eleven! Come on feel the NOIZE!

THE "REALLY HEAVY" METAL BAND

# GARFIELD
## ON
# HOT SAUCE

**L**ife's spicy pleasures are the best. And nothing instantly spices up bland, boring food like hot sauce. That's right—it don't mean a thing if it ain't got that zing!

Sure, it has to be hot, but more importantly, it has to taste good (the hottest isn't always the "bestest"): After I eat the heat, I wanna savor the flavor.

Habañero is the hottest, but Thai, cayenne, jalapeño, chipotle, or any number of other peppers can be used to create palate-pleasin' hot sauces. Blend in different herbs, fruits, and vegetables, and you get endless variety—and variety is the spice of life.

But there's also pleasure—and pain—in the zany names: *Jump Up and Bite Me*; *Lethal Wet Tongue*; *Death Works Overtime*; *Rajun-Cajun Rump Roaster*. I just made those up, but there *should* be ones called that. Hey, maybe I'll just have to bottle my own big fat fiery hot sauce!

JALAPEÑO!

CAYENNE!

HABAÑERO!

PERUVIAN DEATH PEPPER!

FOOM

YOU WIN...

THEN WHY AM I NOT HAPPY?

JIM DAVIS 9-17

# GARFIELD ON INSULTS

**S**naps, *caps, put-downs, slams* . . . an insult by any other name is still fun—especially if you're the one dissing it out and not taking it.

Most of my tongue-lashing is tongue-in-cheek, as it's often directed toward lovable losers Jon and Odie, both of whom are unarmed in a battle of wits. If necessary, though, I can reach into my vast arsenal of wisecracks and comebacks and unleash enough verbal firepower to blast any bully or snub any snob.

So, like excuses, insults are your friends. An insult a day will keep dipwads at bay. Is any of this sinking in, Cheese Brain? Yeah, I'm talking to you, Fungus Face. Have you ever considered a career as a crash dummy? By the way, what's that strange growth on your neck? Oh, it's your *head*!

Whoa, I'm sorry. No harm intended; insults are just too inviting. So, please forgive me . . . Litter-Box Breath. Hey, I just couldn't resist a parting shot.

> **You're so stupid, you flunked recess.**

COMING UP NEXT, "THE CAT, NATURE'S SMART ALECK"

WHAT'S ON?

NOTHING THAT WOULD INTEREST YOU, BEAN BRAIN

© 1991 PAWS, INC.

JIM DAVIS 7-12

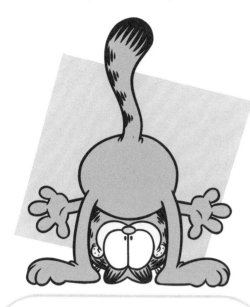

Is that your face,
or did your pants
fall down?

Nice haircut.
Still going to the
dog groomer?

You've got the IQ
of a turnip.

I've seen nicer
teeth in my comb.

# GARFIELD ON LAWYERS

TRUST ME

There's an old joke: What do you call 5,000 lawyers at the bottom of the ocean? Answer: a good start. Here's another one: What do you call a lawyer who doesn't chase ambulances? Retired. And how about one more? How can you tell when a lawyer is lying? His lips are moving.

Okay, okay. So I poke fun at lawyers. What are they gonna do, sue me? But when all is said and done, I guess the legal profession is a valid one. I mean, not everyone's bright enough to go to medical school, right?

THE TIMES THEY ARE A-CHANGIN'

BEWARE OF THE DOG'S LAWYER

© 1991 PAWS, INC. All Rights Reserved.

HEY, CAT!

THIS IS MY LAWYER, SID. I HAVE A RESTRAINING ORDER AGAINST YOU!

UH, WHY THE SMILE?

I'VE NEVER SQUISHED A LAWYER

© 2004 PAWS, INC. All Rights Reserved.

# GARFIELD
## ON
# LAZINESS

Some call it "laziness"; I call it "deep thought." Some say, "Go for it"; I say, "Make it come to you." But, personally, I don't even consider myself lazy: I'm just motivationally challenged.

Okay, who am I kidding? I'm the poster cat for laziness. I'm the sultan of sloth. I'm so lazy, I take coffee breaks between naps.

Yes, I'm just a big fat ol' doily on the recliner of life—and that's the way I like it. Hey, life's more fun when you take it lying down.

He only chases arthritic mice.

He hired another cat to shed for him.

WHOO₀₀₀... ONE...
He thinks breathing is an exercise.

**Garfield is sooooo lazy...**

He makes Jon buy pre-shredded drapes.

He doesn't walk in his sleep... he hitchhikes.

He has a doorman open the refrigerator for him.

# GARFIELD ON
# LITERARY CLASSICS

**D**on Quixote, Madame Bovary, Moby-Dick, Ulysses . . . these are some of the great books of world literature. They're great for exploring universal themes of the human condition such as good and evil, love and hate, truth, faith, honor, and culture. They're also great for squashing large, hairy spiders. (Russian novels are especially deadly. In fact, a copy of *The Brothers Karamazov* could crush a raccoon, if it didn't bore it to death first.)

Don't get me wrong. I'm a big supporter of the classics—especially in comic-book form. Hey, what can I say? *Moby-Dick* is a whale of a tale, but reading this ponderous thousand-page novel would leave me blubbering. But I loved the Mr. Magoo cartoon! And the film version with Gregory Peck was okay, too. But I digress. Or maybe not. Maybe *I* should create my own kooky classics? I'd make a great "Tomcat Sawyer," "Furry Potter," or "Munchcat of Notre Dame!"

*DIGEST ANY GOOD BOOKS LATELY?*

A TALE OF TWO KITTIES

**Beauty and the Feast**

The Three Munchketeers

**WAR & PIZZA**

CHICKS LIKE INTELLECTUAL GUYS

SO I'M BONING UP ON CLASSIC LITERATURE

"HERE'S MR. BUTTERFLY, VISITING MISS DAISY...."

THE MAN'S READING A COLORING BOOK

JIM DAVIS 7-1

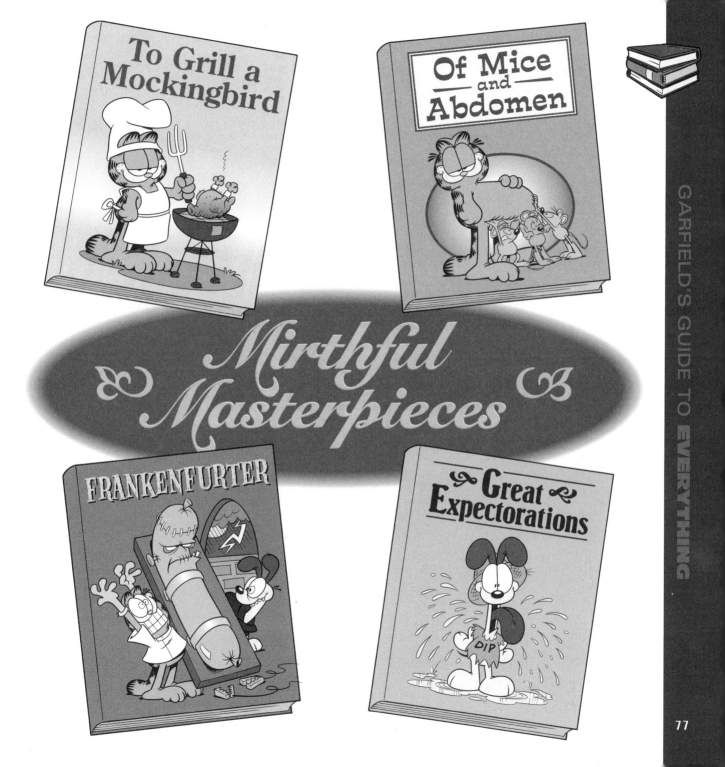

To Grill a Mockingbird

Of Mice and Abdomen

Mirthful Masterpieces

FRANKENFURTER

Great Expectorations

**L**ove, sweet love. What is this many splendored thing that conquers all, makes fools of us all, and makes the world go 'round?

More has been written about love than about any other subject. Poets, playwrights, and songwriters have explored the mysteries of this enigmatic emotion and rhapsodized over its awesome power. Love has been characterized as everything from malady to madness, from an itch in the heart to a pain in the brain. Love can be at first sight—or blind. It can be two hearts beating as one or one song sung by two. It can even be a score of zero in tennis.

All this ethereal, esoteric stuff adds up to a headache for me. I prefer to keep it simple. I love my friends, my food, and myself (though not necessarily in that order). I believe in love at first bite. And that true love is sharing the last piece of pizza!

**E**ver since Dr. Frankenstein stitched together a monster from various bodies robbed from graves, the mad scientist has gotten a bad rap. They're painted as raving lunatics, but these guys actually make science fun. The regular scientist studies germs and develops vaccines. Bor-ing! The mad scientist uses radiation to create gigantic mutated insects and puts the brain of a gorilla into the body of a pretty girl. Now THAT'S a science project every kid would want to try!

## DR. FRANKENSTEIN'S PET PEEVES

⚡ Igor always comes back with wrong brain

⚡ Insanely high electric bill

⚡ Angry villagers always trying to burn down castle; can't get affordable home-owners insurance

⚡ Popularity of cremation means fewer graves available for robbing

⚡ Monster never calls on Father's Day

But being a mad scientist isn't all grave-robbing and glory. Things can go wrong. Your creature can turn on you; the giant laser you've constructed to melt the polar ice cap can run out of power; or a rival mad scientist can put YOUR brain into the body of a gorilla. Occupational hazards notwithstanding, these creative thinkers should be saluted, because the mad science of today is the medical marvel of tomorrow!

# GARFIELD ON MARRIAGE

I'm one of the world's most eligible bachelors; and after all these years, it's pretty clear that I'm going to stay that way. But it's not because there aren't a bevy of babes eager to tie the knot with me.

Arlene is the most obvious one to be the lucky winner of the Garfield love sweepstakes. But what if she snores? And what if her mother moves in? And what if her mother snores?! Not to mention that Pooky would be insanely jealous. Besides, I need my fridge space.

Yeah, I know those are just excuses. The real reason I won't marry Arlene is because I'm deeply in love with someone else—me.

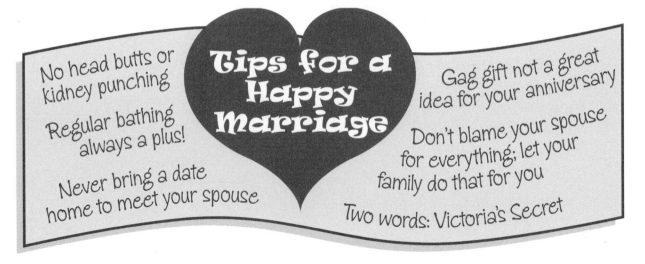

## Tips for a Happy Marriage

No head butts or kidney punching

Regular bathing always a plus!

Never bring a date home to meet your spouse

Gag gift not a great idea for your anniversary

Don't blame your spouse for everything; let your family do that for you

Two words: Victoria's Secret

# GARFIELD
### ON
# MICE

**S**ome cats love munching on mice. That's never been my thing. As I've always said, "Show me a good mouser, and I'll show you a cat with bad breath." Plus, chasing them expends way too much energy. But I *can* catch a mouse . . . provided you throw it right to me.

Actually, I'm not sure how this whole cat-and-mouse thing got started. It's true that we cats are natural hunters, but I'd much rather stalk a herd of wild donuts than some plague germm with feet.

But I have an understanding with the mice in Jon's house: I don't eat them . . . and they don't booby-trap the litter box.

# GARFIELD
## ON
# MONDAYS

The "M" word. The armpit of days. Mondays.

Although I don't work or go to school, I still dread Mondays. In fact, I never met a Monday I didn't hate. For me, they're all about pain. Like flossing an angry wolverine . . . with gingivitis.

One Monday, I wished for a fifty-pound pan of lasagna—it landed on me. Another Monday, I found six crickets synchronized-swimming in my water bowl. Then there was the ugly incident of the land mine in my breakfast. (Can you say "KA-BLOOEY!"?) And "Diet Monday"? . . . "Vet Monday"? . . . let's not even go there.

It seems there's really only one way for me to beat the Monday curse: go to bed early Sunday night and set my alarm for Tuesday!

# MONDAYS ARE ELIMINATED
## World switches to six-day week!

# GARFIELD
## ON
# MONEY

The apostle Paul said that the love of money is the root of all evil. The playwright and wit George Bernard Shaw said the *lack* of money is the root of all evil. I'll bet they're both right . . . but I won't put any money on it.

We all know money makes the world go 'round; and if it's an evil, it's a necessary one. Life's necessities—food, clothing, shelter, cable TV—aren't free (unless you're a pet. And humans think *they're* superior).

Let's face it: Everyone would like to win the lottery, and I'm no different. But don't worry; I'd make good use of the money. I wouldn't just spend it on myself. I'd start by buying Jon a personality and sending Odie to a clinic for problem droolers. I'd even donate to a charity (Mothers Against Dogs Driving is one of my favorites). *Then* I'd do some things for myself.

YOU CAN'T BE TOO RICH OR TOO RESTED

## THINGS GARFIELD WOULD DO IF HE WON THE LOTTERY

$ A refrigerator in every room!

$ Build a stall around his litter box

$ Hire some goon to rough up the neighborhood dogs

$ Get petted by a different babe every night

$ Have his stomach enlarged

$ Get a job, just so he could quit it

$ Eat, sleep, and look rich doing it!

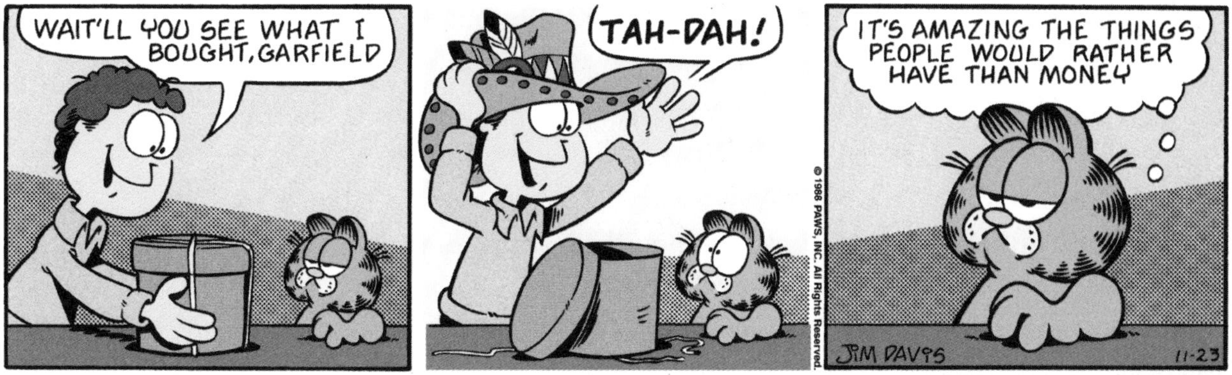
WAIT'LL YOU SEE WHAT I BOUGHT, GARFIELD
TAH-DAH!
IT'S AMAZING THE THINGS PEOPLE WOULD RATHER HAVE THAN MONEY
JIM DAVIS 11-23
© 1988 PAWS, INC. All Rights Reserved.

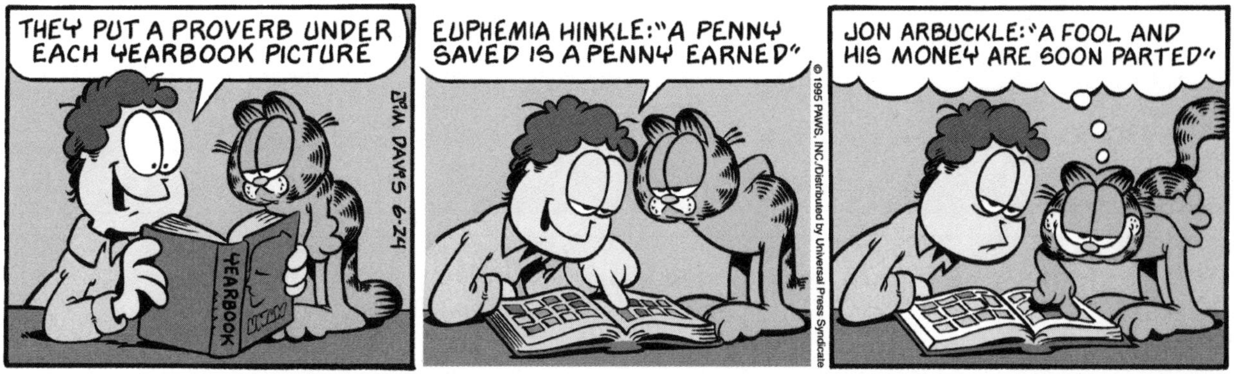
THEY PUT A PROVERB UNDER EACH YEARBOOK PICTURE
YEARBOOK
JIM DAVIS 6-24
EUPHEMIA HINKLE: "A PENNY SAVED IS A PENNY EARNED"
JON ARBUCKLE: "A FOOL AND HIS MONEY ARE SOON PARTED"
© 1995 PAWS, INC./Distributed by Universal Press Syndicate

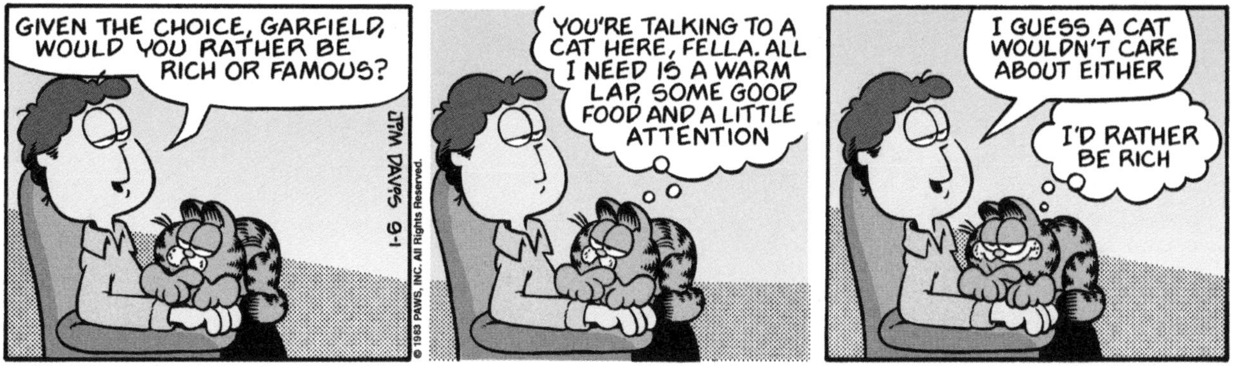
GIVEN THE CHOICE, GARFIELD, WOULD YOU RATHER BE RICH OR FAMOUS?
JIM DAVIS 9-1
YOU'RE TALKING TO A CAT HERE, FELLA. ALL I NEED IS A WARM LAP, SOME GOOD FOOD AND A LITTLE ATTENTION
I GUESS A CAT WOULDN'T CARE ABOUT EITHER
I'D RATHER BE RICH
© 1983 PAWS, INC. All Rights Reserved.

# GARFIELD ON MONSTERS

**W**erewolves, mummies, zombies—they don't frighten me a bit. Nope, the only thing that scares me is running out of lasagna. In fact, I love monsters; especially the ones that Jon dates. And when it comes to the silver screen, I really prefer the classic creatures to these current slice-and-dice guys. Anyone can put on a hockey mask and carve up a summer camp. The old monsters had class. They had style. Hey, Dracula even wore a tuxedo!

But it's been quite a while since we've heard from the sinister stars of yesteryear. Whatever happened to them? Funny you should ask . . .

86

BURP

# WHATEVER HAPPENED TO...

## CREATURE FROM THE BLACK LAGOON
Lost starring role in tuna fish commercial when he ate the director

## WOLF MAN
Career sidelined by severe male-pattern baldness

## FRANKENSTEIN'S MONSTER
Created a line of slightly irregular big & tall clothing

## DRACULA
Ballooned to 250 pounds; had to switch to low-cholesterol plasma

## INVISIBLE MAN
Hasn't been seen onscreen in over fifty years; currently doing voice-over work

PLASMA LO-CAL

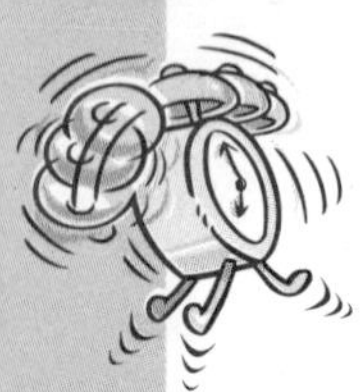

# GARFIELD ON MORNINGS

I'm a surly riser; I rise and whine. I just can't get up for mornings; they're the worst way to start the day. To me, a good morning is any one you sleep through. Because let's face it—waking up is hard to do. That's why some sadist invented alarm clocks (which were made to be broken).

I don't get the whole "morning person" thing. As far as I'm concerned, people who get up at the crack of dawn are cracked. And the early bird oughta get his head examined! What's so great about getting the worms?

Besides, seen one sunrise, seen 'em all. If it's that amazing, someone can tape it, and you can watch it later. Just listen to your inner slug, and remember: Anything worth doing can be done after lunch.

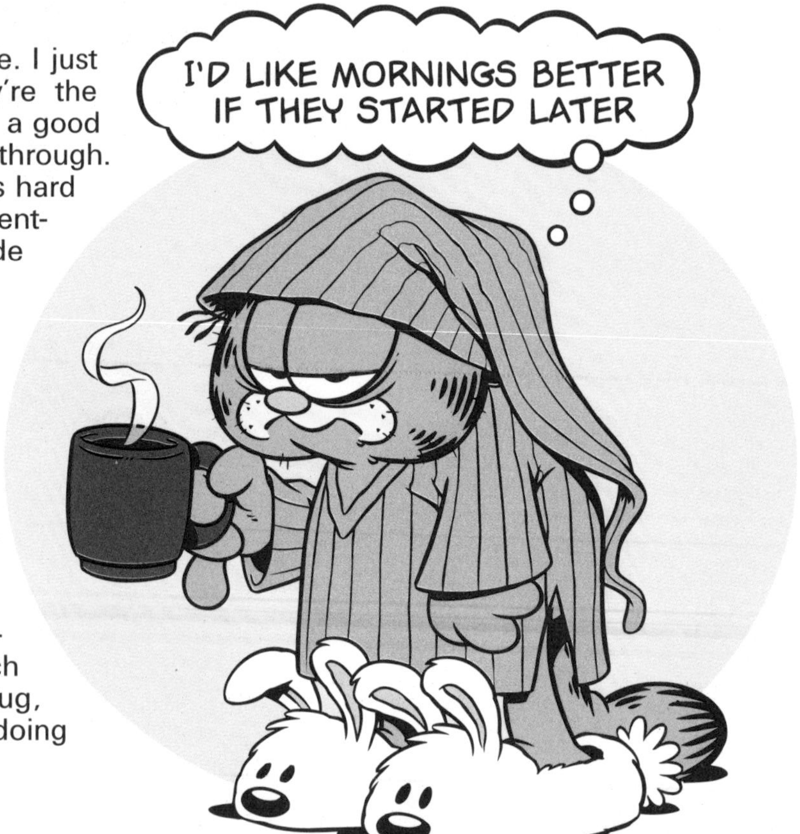
I'D LIKE MORNINGS BETTER IF THEY STARTED LATER

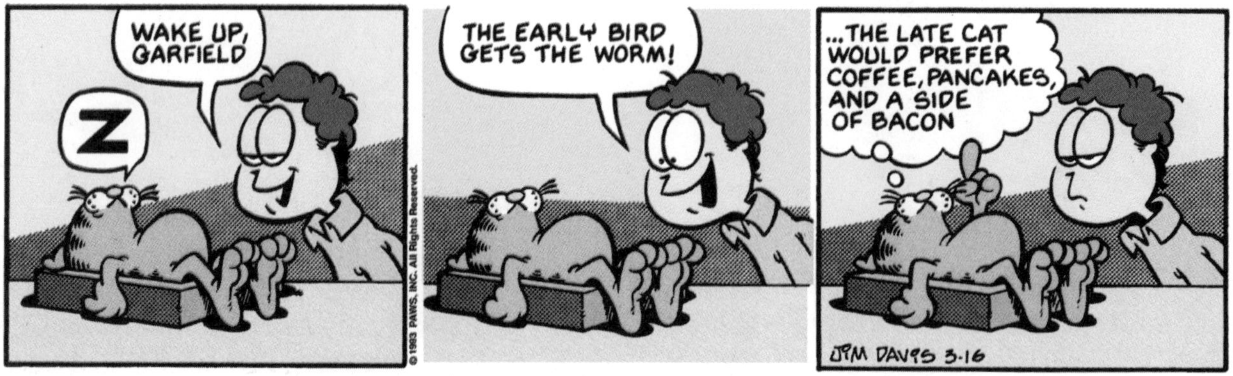
WAKE UP, GARFIELD
Z
THE EARLY BIRD GETS THE WORM!
...THE LATE CAT WOULD PREFER COFFEE, PANCAKES, AND A SIDE OF BACON
© 1993 PAWS, INC. All Rights Reserved.
JIM DAVIS 3-16

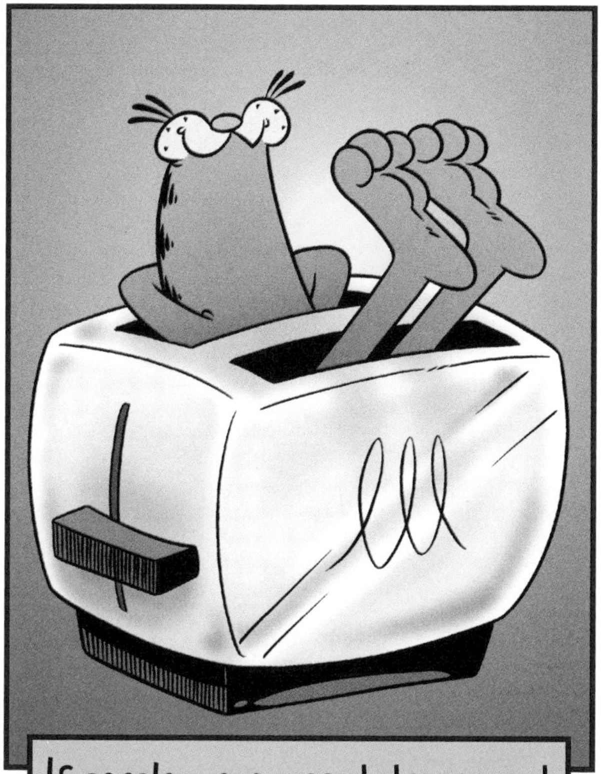

If people were meant to pop out of bed, we'd all sleep in toasters

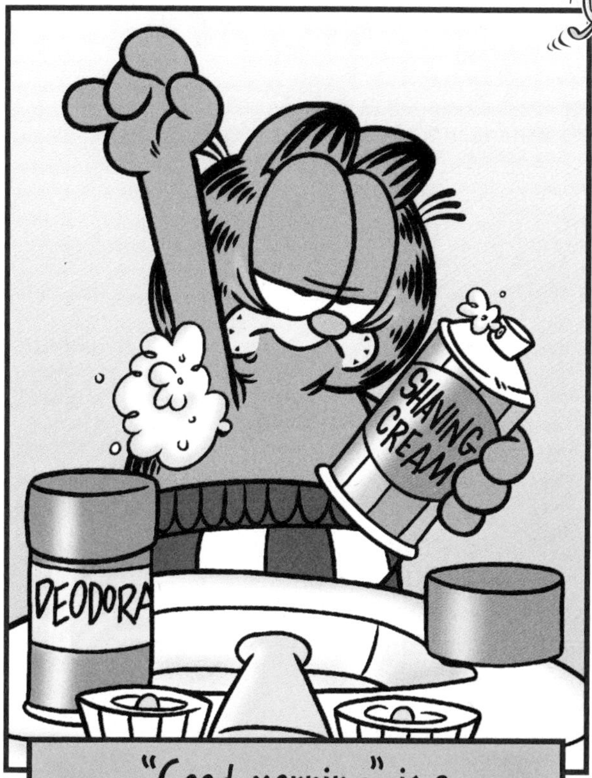
SHAVING CREAM
DEODORA

"Good morning" is a contradiction in terms

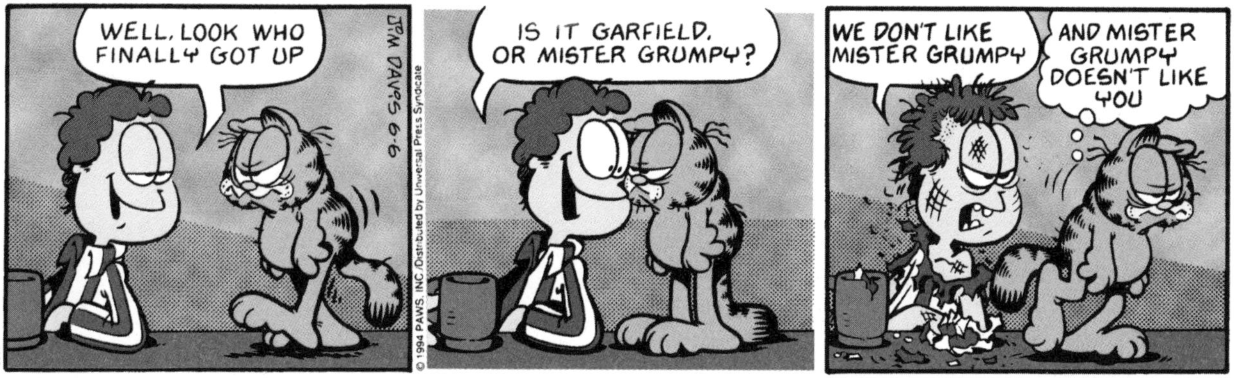
WELL, LOOK WHO FINALLY GOT UP
JIM DAVIS 6-6
© 1994 PAWS, INC./Distributed by Universal Press Syndicate
IS IT GARFIELD, OR MISTER GRUMPY?
WE DON'T LIKE MISTER GRUMPY
AND MISTER GRUMPY DOESN'T LIKE YOU

# GARFIELD ON **MOVIES**

WHAT I REALLY WANT TO DO IS DIRECT

I admit it. I'm a movie junkie. I love films of all genres: comedies, dramas, thrillers, sci-fi, horror, foreign, independent, mysteries—even the occasional musical. (But don't tell anyone. I've got a rep to protect.) However, I won't mindlessly munch my popcorn and watch just anything. You couldn't pay me to sit through a weepy love story, and I definitely don't do documentaries.

And while I'm a certified film fanatic, I'm a little dismayed at how movies have changed over the years. Nowadays, everything is driven by test audiences and marketing. *Citizen Kane*, one of the greatest films of all time, probably couldn't get made today. The studios would want to make the main character a teenager, add some car chases and cleavage, toss in a few explosions, and maybe even Jackie Chan. I shudder at the very thought of it.

Luckily, not everything that comes out of Tinseltown is tripe. There are still a lot of fine films released every year. And as long as Hollywood can muster up some genuine movie magic, I'll be there at the multiplex with my jumbo bucket of popcorn. Extra butter and salt, of course.

SO, JON, WHAT MOVIE ARE WE SEEING?

"SLUDGE MONSTER VII: THE OOZING"

WOULD YOU LIKE A BUCKET OF POPCORN?

NO, JUST THE BUCKET, PLEASE

# LIGHTS, CAMERA, LAUGHTER!

Here's my take on some of the greats of the silver screen . . .

# GARFIELD ON NERDS

They're also known as geeks, freaks, dweebs, dorks, or doofuses. But a nerd by any other name would be just as socially inept.

Where do you find a nerd? Usually in his mom's basement. Or at the comic-book store. Or wearing plastic Vulcan ears at the local Star Trek convention.

I'm an expert on these strange alien life-forms. After all, my owner, Jon Arbuckle, is a nerd. In fact, he's "Nerdzilla," king of all nerds. His idea of Friday night fun is yodeling in a kilt while riding a unicycle.

But not all nerds are losers (like Jon). Some can grow up to be successful computer geeks (like billionaire Bill Gates). And nerds provide a valuable service: They give high school football players someone to beat up.

## NERD PICKUP LINES

- "Your eyes sparkle like the fairy wings of Alwyn, pixie queen of Hypathia . . ."
- "Haven't we battled before at a Dungeons and Dragons tournament?"
- "Hey, baby! How about my mom drives us to the comic-book store?"
- "You're so pretty . . . I wish I had an action figure of you!"
- "Wanna get together later for a Vulcan Mind Meld?"

# YOU KNOW YOU'RE A NERD WHEN...

You think playing the accordion makes you look "hot"

In school, you were voted "Most Likely to Marry a Kitchen Appliance"

You own an extensive collection of bunny slippers

The last CD you bought was "Best of the Harmonicats"

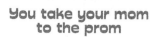

You take your mom to the prom

You alphabetize your sock drawer

# GARFIELD
## ON
# NOBEL PRIZES

The Nobel Prize is an illustrious award (mucho kudos and ca$h!) given annually to luminaries since 1901. Yet, during all that time, no cat—including yours truly—has ever won it. It's a crime, but one which probably won't ever be punished.

My chances are hurt because the awards are only given for achievements in a restrictive group of categories: chemistry, physics, medicine, peace, literature, economics. Well, HELLO, ever think of adding some new ones? (Sleeping? Hairballs?) But that's okay . . . I can do science: I once devised a method to break into the fridge without leaving my bed! (Appetite is the mother of invention.)

I know part of the problem: Alfred Nobel, who established the prizes through his will, was Swedish. He was also the inventor of dynamite (which is why he needed a will). Meanwhile, I once mooned Abba during a command performance for the King of Sweden. You don't have to be a Nobel winner to do the math.

**In the future, new Nobel Prize categories will include Virtual Physics, Biospherics, and Biggest Watermelon.**

SANTA CLAUS ISN'T STUPID, YOU KNOW!

I'D THINK TWICE BEFORE SENDING HIM THAT LETTER ABOUT HOW GOOD YOU WERE THIS YEAR!

JIM DAVIS 12-13

MAYBE I SHOULD TAKE OUT THAT PART ABOUT WINNING THE NOBEL PEACE PRIZE

REALLY?! CAN I SHAKE YOUR HAND?

# GARFIELD
## ON
# OLYMPICS

The ancient Greeks contributed two very important things to Western civilization: baklava and the Olympics.

How did these famous games get started? One Greek legend says that the mighty Herakles (or Hercules, as we know him) won a race at Olympia and then decreed that the race should be re-enacted every four years. Who knows if that's true? But we do know this: Athletes in the earliest games ran in the nude, making them the very first streakers.

The modern Olympic Games include track and field, gymnastics, swimming, wrestling, weightlifting, and other unexciting events. If I were in charge, things would be a lot different . . .

## GARFIELD'S SUGGESTIONS FOR NEW OLYMPIC EVENTS

★ The dogput
★ Synchronized snoring
★ Speedsnacking
★ Mice hockey
★ Fridge lift
★ Hairball hack
★ Eat till you explode!

# GARFIELD ON PARTIES

**S**ome people believe in the two-party system—one on Friday and one on Saturday. I believe in partying every day! Ooga Chaka! I'm a wild 'n' crazy cat . . . a true party animal! I like to party till the cows come home! Then party with the cows! *Then* party till the cows call the cops!

I believe in serious partying where you check your brain at the door! I believe it's our patriotic duty to party . . . from the twilight's last gleaming to the dawn's early light! I believe in seeking new party frontiers: We must boldly party where no one has partied before! I believe in rocking the Casbah (whether Sharif likes it or not)! I believe I *am* the party!

## PARTY PLEDGE

I, Garfield, do solemnly, yet with some giggling, vow to preserve, protect, and propagate the true spirit of partying by celebrating whenever and wherever possible; and to attain and uphold my bad reputation as a party animal though affronts to common decency and otherwise fun behavior; which, if I don't, may I spend the rest of my life chained to someone who thinks maggots are "really interesting."

## REASONS TO PARTY

- Your place could use a good trashing
- A party demon has possessed your body
- You just like to make ice
- You can't think of anything boring to do
- You have an overactive party gland
- Haven't annoyed your neighbors in a while
- You have a sudden urge to "limbo"
- Good way to meet your local law enforcement officials

IF THE LAMPSHADE FITS, WEAR IT!

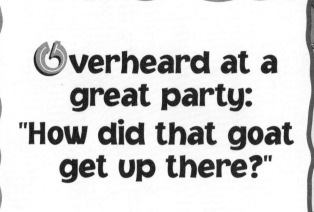**O**verheard at a great party: "How did that goat get up there?"

**O**verheard at a great party: "I love the way this dip squishes between my toes."

**L**et's get something straight: Cats are not pets. We don't belong to humans; we merely tolerate you and allow you to serve us. Got it?

In fact, I don't understand this whole master-pet thing, anyway. We animals eat for free, shed on your furniture, stain your carpet, make you clean up our poop . . . and *you're* the superior species? Yeah, right.

But if you insist on turning your home into a zoo, let me give you a little advice about the pet set . . .

**Goldfish:** Neat, quiet, and they make a tasty hors d'oeuvre!

**Parrots:** You can teach them to do anything . . . except shut up!

**Iguanas:** Definitely not party animals. A pet rock has more personality than these reptilian rejects.

**Ferrets:** Cousin to the skunk and weasel, here's a critter that only Ellie May Clampett could love.

**Rabbits:** Buy two chocolate ones and hope they multiply.

**Guinea pigs:** Sure, they're cute . . . but they're a lousy source of bacon.

# GARFIELD
## ON
# PLASTIC SURGERY

**P**lastic surgery . . . it's not just for Hollywood anymore! America is in the midst of a makeover obsession, with regular Joes—and, more often, Joanns—going to extremes to transform themselves from ugly ducklings to beautiful swans (or, at least, "swannabees").

Personally, I'm kind of creeped out by this Frankenstein stuff. Brow lifts, liposuction, skin bleaching, Botox injections . . . what's next—a head transplant? Of course, that's easy for me to say: I'm a paragon of feline studliness. I like me just the way I am.

But I also respect other people's rights to change their looks however they see fit. America is the land of the free and the home of the babes, so if you want to glam it up and reinvent yourself, that's your prerogative. And, let's face it, some faces could use a little work: a tongue tuck for Odie, hair plugs for Ziggy, a beak job for Opus—to name and defame but a few. As for *moi*, I'll pass, thank you. The only thing of mine going under the knife is my sixteen-ounce T-bone steak!

# GARFIELD
## ON
# PORK

**A**h . . . the other white meat. I'm a little piggie when it comes to pork. I love it in all its permutations: breaded, barbecued, deep-fried; as ribs, chops, roasts, or ham; ground in a hot dog, sliced on a pizza, shredded in a taco. I'd even eat it frozen on a stick (porksicles, anyone?).

Pork isn't just the tastiest of meats; it's also the funniest. Beef? Lamb? Veal? See? Not funny. Chicken is funny, though. It's a close second to pork. Watch how adding the word "pork" gives these entrees extra flair: Pork à la King, Pork Wellington, Pork Cordon Bleu, Pork Cacciatore, Pork Scampi, Pork Dijonaise, Pork à la Mode. I could go on and on.

So let them say what they will about pork. Let doctors and dieticians impugn it for being fatty and salty and high in cholesterol. I don't care. If loving pork is wrong, I don't want to be right.

OINK! OINK!

THAT WAS MRS. BROWN ON THE PHONE

SHE SAYS YOU BIT HER

WELL?!   SHE WAS WEARING A MUMU WITH PORK CHOPS PRINTED ALL OVER IT

JIM DAVIS 2-3

© 2000 PAWS, INC. /Distributed by Universal Press Syndicate

# GARFIELD
## ON
# PSYCHICS

**C**an someone really predict the future? Lots of people claim to. They use tarot cards, crystal balls, astrology, numerology, channeling, past life regression, palmistry—and other equally scientific methods.

But the ones I like best are the telephone psychics. You know the type. They advertise on TV with names like Psychic Pals Network and offer to tell your future—for only $2.95 a minute. You don't have to be Nostradamus to predict what your future will bring: a gigantic phone bill.

Fake psychics are always looking for suckers, but don't fall into their trap. How can you avoid getting conned? Read on . . .

## TIPS FOR SPOTTING A PHONY PSYCHIC

- Asks to read your credit cards instead of tarot cards
- Uses bowling ball instead of crystal ball
- Thinks channeling is something you do with the remote control
- Tries to contact the dead but claims to get busy signal

# GARFIELD ON
# SHAKESPEARE

**W**hen it comes to writers, William "The Bard" Shakespeare is a heavyweight (something I appreciate). This literary giant racked up plays, poems, and sonnets like basketball giant Wilt "The Stilt" Chamberlain did points, rebounds, and girlfriends.

Shakespeare wrote things 400 years ago that are still used in the language today. In fact, he coined over 1,500 words and phrases, including the words "puke" and "puppy dog," which I'm sure were created together. ("Hamlet's cat puked when he saw the new puppy dog.")

Everyone probably knows a line from Shakespeare, even if they don't know it: "To be, or not to be . . . ," "To thine own self be true," "Neither a borrower nor a lender be." And these are all just from *Hamlet* (a play about a dithering Danish prince who creates a royal mess when he decides to buy a puppy dog).

All the world's a stage . . . and I've waxed Shakespearean myself many times over the years, uttering my own notable, quotable lines:

# GARFIELD ON SHOW BUSINESS

**L**ike any great performer, I love an audience . . . even a hostile one. And, believe me, I've faced—and been hit in the face by—some tough crowds over the years during my gigs on the neighborhood fence.

Naturally, I've been the target of the standard boos, taunts, and rotten tomatoes. But I've also been the recipient of more cruel and unusual punishment: A toy cat was hung in effigy; a geezer hit me with his dentures; once, I was even shaved while performing at a barber convention! Nowadays, I consider a good crowd one that doesn't wake up. But at least I'm starting to attract a better class of heckler: I've been hit with an empty caviar tin and an Italian shoe!

Yet, like any good trouper, I know the show must go on. So, even though my act elicits more brickbats than bravos, I continue to perform. And why shouldn't I? If William Hung can make it, anyone can. Besides, I don't just sing; I also dance, do stand-up comedy, even a little magic: I'm a veritable Renaissance cat. Cue the spotlight: I just might have to take my act on the road and become an American idol!

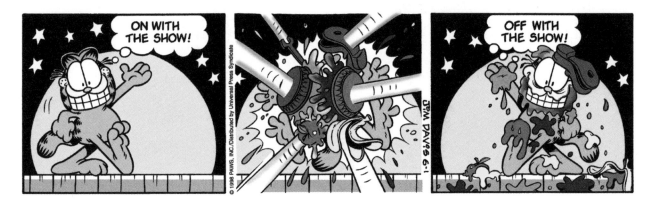

# GARFIELD ON SLEEP

**S**leep: We all do it; some of us just do it better than others. Me, I'm a master practitioner . . . I've got a Ph.D. in ZZZZZs. (It's so easy, I can do it with my eyes closed.)

I don't just catnap; I hibernate. (Sleep is the best eighteen hours of my day.) I like to take *two hundred* and forty winks. When I saw logs, they're redwoods!

Sleep is blissful slumber . . . the natural way to gork out. It's the best defense against mornings, and the perfect way to waste a day. It's also the stuff dreams are made of. I could go on rhapsodizing and extolling its virtues, but I feel a nap attack coming on. I think it's time for a snoozzzzzzzzz . . .

# YOU KNOW YOU'RE DREAMING WHEN

## THEY CHOOSE "THE 10 SEXIEST PEOPLE EVER" AND THEY'RE ALL YOU

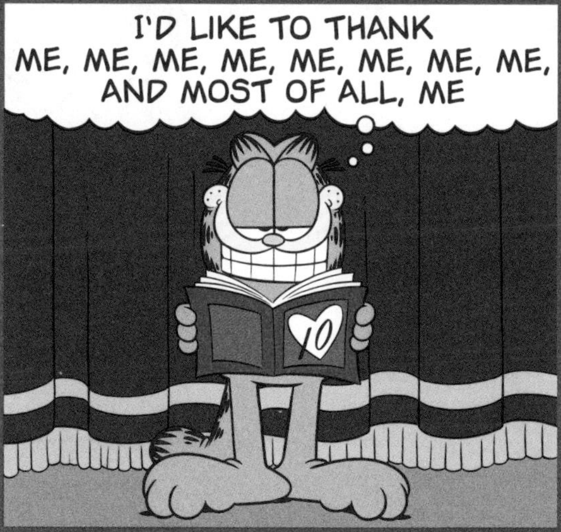
I'D LIKE TO THANK ME, ME, ME, ME, ME, ME, ME, ME, AND MOST OF ALL, ME
10

## YOU GET TO THROW PEOPLE IN THE DUNGEON

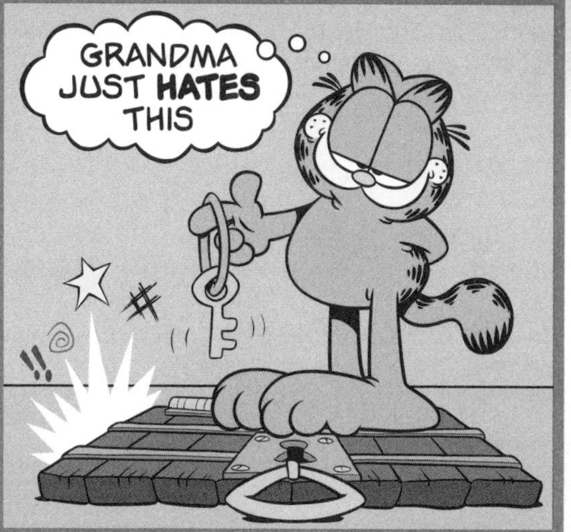
GRANDMA JUST **HATES** THIS

## THEY ANNOUNCE THAT CHOCOLATE IS A DIET FOOD

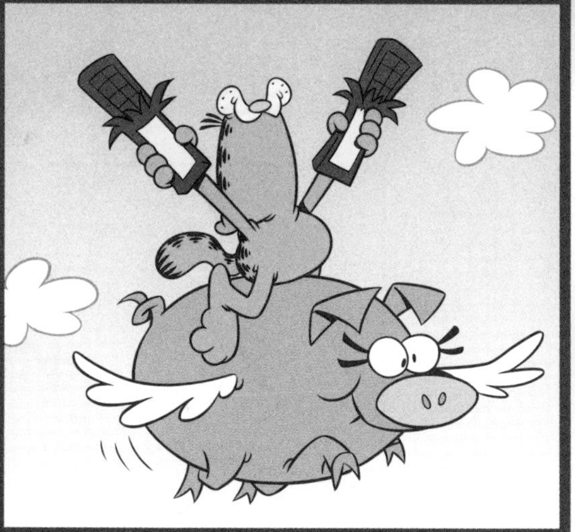

## YOU'RE UP TO YOUR EYEBALLS IN MONEY

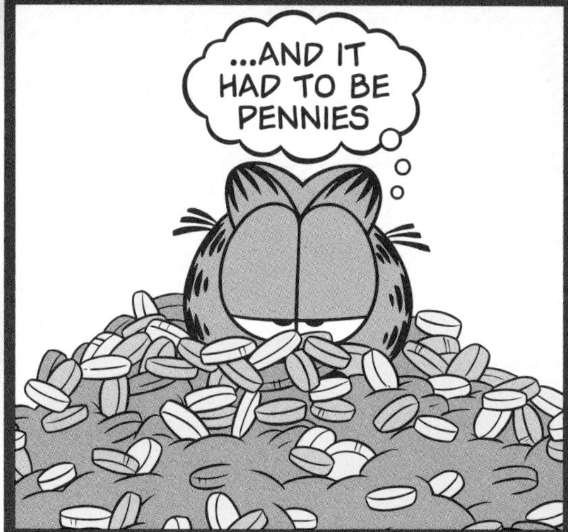
...AND IT HAD TO BE PENNIES

# GARFIELD
## ON
# SPIDERS

**U**gh. The very word gives me the willies. Call it an extreme case of arachnophobia, but I can't stand those eight-legged freaks. They're hairy, they're creepy, and they're just plain ugly. But I'll give them this: They make a great sound when you squish them.

Some of my more "sensitive" fans have written to me about my spider-whacking. They protest my so-called "brutal treatment of our arachnid brothers and sisters." They say that most kinds of spiders are completely harmless. I agree; especially the dead kinds!

You want to know the REAL reason I whack spiders?
I'll tell you. I tried eating one once, but it tasted yucky.

# GARFIELD ON STUPIDITY

**L**et's face it: As a nation—no, as a *species*—we're dumb and getting dumber. People are eating a big bowl of stupid for breakfast with a side order of folly. Soon, the average person will be less intelligent than his or her toaster.

I'm serious. Are you familiar with the Darwin Awards, which dubiously honor people who have removed themselves from the gene pool by acts of stupendous stupidity? Seemingly every day, somewhere on the planet, some idiot is juggling live hand grenades or performing some other fatally funny "stupid human trick."

Or just turn on the tube and watch some boob stick his tongue into a beehive. You'd swear Albert Einstein was watching *Fear Factor* when he said, "Only two things are infinite—the universe and human stupidity, and I'm not so sure about the universe."

I can relate. I see "stoopidity" rear its goofy head every day at home with Odie and Jon. I'm telling you, if space aliens landed at our place, they'd report no intelligent life on Earth!

MAY I SPEAK TO THE MORON OF THE HOUSE?

COULD YOU BE MORE SPECIFIC?

JIM DAVIS 6-26

© 1998 PAWS, INC./Distributed by Universal Press Syndicate

# GARFIELD
## ON
# SUPERHEROES

**F**aster than a speeding hairball! More powerful than dog breath! Able to eat a pizza the size of a football field! It's Garfield-Man!

I admit it. I've always wanted to be a superhero: fighting bad guys, flying around the city, having a youthful ward as a sidekick. But I wouldn't have one of those lame secret identities where I put on a pair of glasses and suddenly nobody knows who I am. Hello? Superman? Glasses? Not the best way to completely hide your identity. I mean, how unobservant is Lois Lane? No, if I were a superhero, I'd want to be more like Batman: a billionaire with a secret cave and a really hot ride.

My villains would be very colorful, too. There'd be the Deadly Drool Bucket, the evil Dr. Port-o-Let, and the Supreme Stinkinator—part man, part skunk. Of course, like all superheroes, I'd have my weakness, that one thing that would render me powerless: catnip!

BEHOLD! EARTH'S MIGHTIEST SANDWICH!

LOOK, UP IN THE SKY! IT'S A BIRD! IT'S A PLANE!

NO! IT'S...

WHOP!

SUPER POOKY!

JIM DAVIS 10-9

# GARFIELD ON TATTOOS

Here's what I have to say to all those crazy nuts covered in tattoos: Just wait till you're sixty. You ever see a sixty-year-old person? They're flabby and wrinkly. How are those cool dragons and flaming skulls gonna look when you're shriveled up like a prune? Not a pretty sight.

But I'm not against all tattoos. In fact, I've even considered getting one. It would have to be something special that really makes a statement, though. Something like "Born to eat bacon," or "My owner is a dork."

Speaking of my dorky owner, Jon, he's the one who could really use a few tattoos to liven up his personality . . .

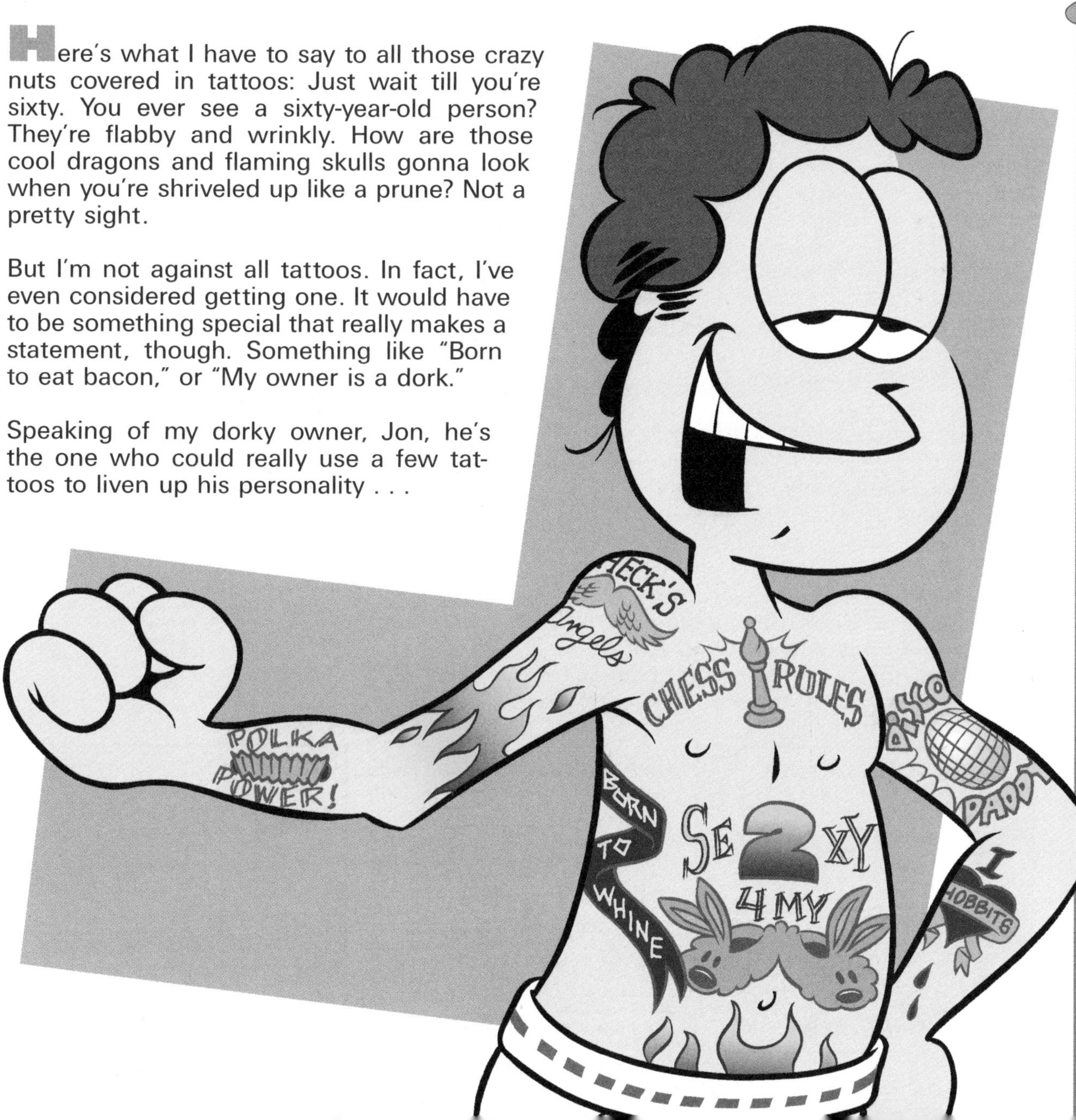
HECK'S Angels
POLKA POWER!
CHESS RULES
DISCO DADDY
BORN TO WHINE
SE2XY 4 MY
I HOBBITS

# GARFIELD
## ON
# TEDDY BEARS

**F**riends may come and friends may go, but a teddy bear is forever. Hey, I'm not ashamed to admit I love my Pooky (that's what I call my teddy bear extraordinaire). So what's not to love? He's the perfect companion: cute, cuddly, understanding, and always there when I need him. Plus, he never tries to hog my blanket or my food. And if I have garlic breath and want to snuggle . . . not a problem.

I can share my deepest thoughts—and deepest sleeps—with Pooky. But what I won't do is share Pooky with anyone else. One time I found him warm to the touch—and it wasn't my touch. I accused him of hugging around, but it turned out that Jon had just taken him out of the dryer. What can I say? I'm a jealous fool! I just can't bear to share my teddy bear.

IT'S POWER POOKY!
DUH, DUH, DUH,
DUUUUUUUH!

ABLE TO STAVE OFF LONELINESS
IN A SINGLE HUG!

YOU DON'T NEED BIG MUSCLES
TO BE A SUPERHERO

JIM DAVIS 3-6

# GARFIELD
## ON
# TELEMARKETERS

**T**hey call at the most inopportune times (usually during dinner) with irritating sales pitches. It's like, if you wanted to change your long-distance provider, or donate to a charity, or get new siding for your house, you'd do it. You wouldn't need these vermin hassling and harassing you about it. If you're like most people, you've tried caller ID, call-blocking, do-not-call lists—anything and everything to stop these phoning nuisances. And still they get through.

Telemarketers are the cockroaches of the sales industry, constantly adapting to their environment and impossible to exterminate. Wouldn't it be great if we could get a list of *their* names and bug *them*? Better yet, in a perfect world, your phone would be equipped with a button that would vaporize these annoying pests!

# GARFIELD
## ON
# TELEVISION

**T**o me, happiness is a warm TV . . . whether I'm asleep on top of it, or watching it till my brain turns to mush. Sure, it's often mindless drivel: implausible plots, sex and violence, catcalls and pratfalls . . . and that's just some of the cartoons!

Television reveals the human condition in all its majesty—and stupidity. Where else can you see real lifesaving surgery alongside (literally, if you have "picture in a picture") a moron gorging himself on Madagascar hissing cockroaches? Truth grosser than fiction.

So, call me a boob-tube tabby, for I willingly wallow in inanity. But I still consider myself a discriminating viewer: I don't do opera, infomercials, spelling bees, and, of course, the Westminster Dog Show. Some of my favorite shows are *Cooking for Klutzes*, *Hairball Theatre*, and *Recycle that Roadkill*.

A handy remote, a bowl of popcorn, and thou, TV.

*In the future, cable TV will be hooked directly into your brain.*

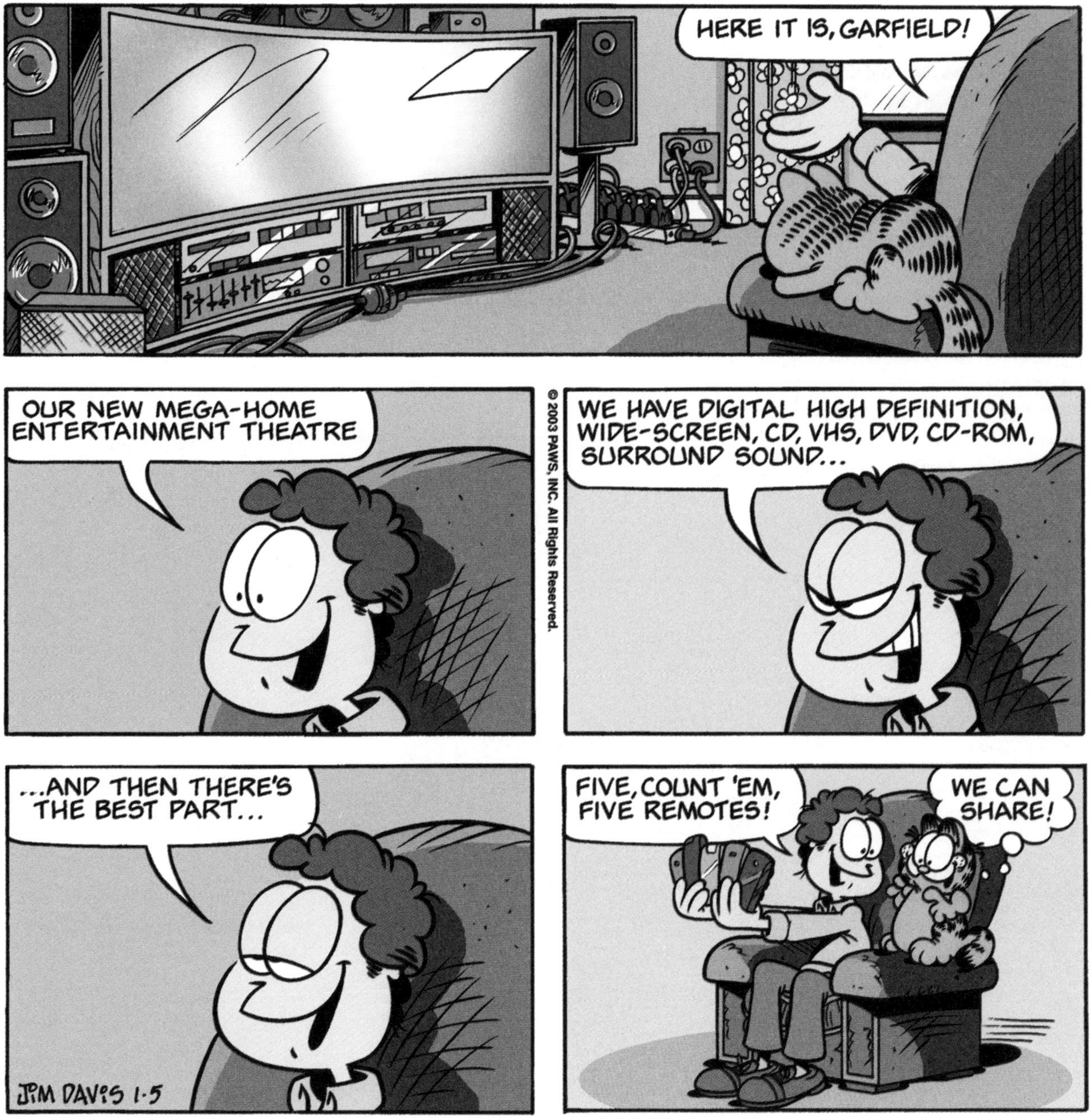
HERE IT IS, GARFIELD!
OUR NEW MEGA-HOME ENTERTAINMENT THEATRE
WE HAVE DIGITAL HIGH DEFINITION, WIDE-SCREEN, CD, VHS, DVD, CD-ROM, SURROUND SOUND...
...AND THEN THERE'S THE BEST PART...
JIM DAVIS 1-5
FIVE, COUNT 'EM, FIVE REMOTES!
WE CAN SHARE!

# GARFIELD
## ON
# THANKSGIVING

Is there any doubt this is one of my favorite holidays? Eating is the real great American pastime, and Thanksgiving is the Super Bowl of Bingeing. Sure, football is also on the menu, but eating till you explode is the true Thanksgiving tradition. Actually, from Turkey Day till New Year's Day, it's just one big, fat holiday feast!

I usually celebrate Thanksgiving with Jon at his parents' house, where, if I'm lucky, his relatives are too bloated to talk. That's not surprising, given the humongous spread his mom puts out. Do we really need *eight* different kinds of potatoes? Of course not, but going overboard on the smorgasbord is part of the fun. Gluttony loves company, so we all dig in and gobble till we wobble! (I'm just thankful the Pilgrims chose turkey instead of possum!)

# GARFIELD'S THANKSGIVING EATING TIPS

Forget silverware and plates; use a shovel and trough.

The best way to eat stuffing is to suck it right out of the bird.

Burp softly and carry a big drumstick.

A heavy feeling in your chest means you've swallowed the tablecloth.

If they can move you without a crane, you didn't eat enough.

You're full when your navel pops out and rockets across the room!

# GARFIELD ON TRAVEL

**S**ome people like to travel the world and visit strange and exotic locations. But who needs the lost luggage, jet lag, and dysentery? When I want to see the world, I pack myself a big snack and click on the Travel Channel. I get to see all kinds of exciting countries and cultures without having to learn a new language, sleep in a strange hotel, or figure out currency conversion. That's my kind of vacation!

Speaking of vacations, I've had more than my share of bad ones (thanks to Jon). The worst was when the "Tightwad Tourist" asked the travel agent for something "tropical and cheap" and we ended up on the island of Guano-Guano. Talk about a bungle in the jungle. The weather was hot and sticky, the hotel didn't have room service, and Jon's underwear became infested with leaf weasels (don't ask!).

I couldn't wait to get home, and I'm definitely staying put for a while. If I ever get the urge to go global, I think I'll just visit the International House of Pancakes.

> HAVE I HAD FUN YET?

Panel 1: WELL, HERE WE ARE IN BEAUTIFUL GUANO-GUANO, GUYS!

Panel 2: LOOK, A NATIVE! ALOHA, DUDE!

Panel 3: ALOHA, THIS! / UH, MUST BE AN OBSCURE GUANO-GUANO GREETING / NO, I THINK THAT'S PRETTY UNIVERSAL

JIM DAVIS 3-27

© 1995 PAWS, INC. All Rights Reserved.

**V**egetarianism is classified as a lifestyle. But I call it a form of insanity, because you'd have to be crazy to give up eating meat. And what's up with tofu? Sure it's fat-free and cholesterol-free. It's also taste-free. It's like snacking on Styrofoam. You can put as many condiments as you like on a piece of Styrofoam, it's still spongy, gross, and inedible.

The lettuce-munchers say that it's wrong to eat anything with a face. That's why I say, fine, don't eat it. Mount it on the wall above the fireplace.

Personally, I can't envision life without beef, chicken, or pork. I'm a natural-born carnivore. (My hero has always been Meat Loaf—the singer and the food.)

So let the veg-heads and soy boys have their cruelty-free cuisine. I'll give up meat when they pry the pork chop from my cold, dead paw.

# GARFIELD
## ON
# VETERINARIANS

know these health-care professionals are a boon to animal-kind . . . but why does every visit to the vet involve poking, prodding, and (shudder) inserting things? It's the twenty-first century. Hasn't someone figured out a better (and less intrusive) way to take a temperature?

Thermometer abuse aside, my veterinarian (or personal physician, as I like to call her) is pretty nice. Jon likes Dr. Liz, too, and drools worse than Odie when he's around her. But she takes it in stride. I guess she's used to dealing with big dumb animals.

### PET PEEVES OF LIZ THE VET

- 🐾 Pathologically shy turtles
- 🐾 Cigar-chomping chimps
- 🐾 Hippos with hemorrhoids
- 🐾 Foul-mouthed parrots
- 🐾 Giraffes with strep throat
- 🐾 Know-it-all owls
- 🐾 Penguins who overdress at casual get-togethers
- 🐾 *Anything* with diarrhea

I HAD THE VET TAKE GARFIELD'S TEMPERATURE

LET'S TALK HEALTH HERE

LET'S TALK DIGNITY HERE

# GARFIELD
## ON
## WORK

I'VE GOT MY "WORK FACE" ON

**D**id you know that the United States has the shortest average vacation time in the "developed" world? Two measly weeks. I've taken naps that long. And a recent poll revealed that nearly half of Americans didn't plan to take any vacation time this year. Now *that's* a national outrage!

And let's not forget our fellow workaholics, the Japanese: They actually have a word, *karoshi*, meaning "death by overwork." That's insane! (Now "death by chocolate" is another matter . . .)

Yeah, I know work is necessary; I just don't want to be the one doing it. And if you want a job as a way to escape your kids, well, that's understandable. But you shouldn't be working your fingers to the bone. Fingers are better used for eating french fries and corn on the cob. Face it: In our workaday world, there's just too much rat race and not enough cheese. (Am I the only one ready for a lunch break?)

YOU DIDN'T DO ANYTHING REMOTELY RESEMBLING WORK TODAY, DID YOU?

WELL, DINNER WAS KIND OF CHEWY

JPM DAV9S 6-25

If this is the gravy train, I must be riding in the caboose.

You really <u>CAN</u> work it off.

Everything gets downsized except the work.

My job is a juggling act...and all my balls just hit the floor.

# GARFIELD
## ON
# WRESTLING

**H**ere's the burning question on everyone's mind: Is professional wrestling real? I'm not sure how this whole thing got started. Why would anyone question this fine sport? Sure, some of the guys have silly names—and even sillier costumes.

And it's true that some of the fighting methods are a little unconventional (you don't find boxers dragging ladders into the ring or smacking each other with folding chairs). But where did people get the idea that everything was rigged?

I can't speak for the steroid boys. Maybe they're faking it. But if I were a wrestler, I'd keep it real! I'd be the Bulkster, the round mound of mayhem! And when I stepped into the ring, face-to-face with my fleabag opponent, Bad 2D Bone, the fur would really fly!

FEEL THE PAIN, BONE BRAIN!

# GARFIELD
## ON
# YOGA

Celebrities from Cameron Diaz to Sting are doing it, but what exactly is it? Yoga comes from Hindu philosophy and means "union"; the union between mind and body, and to a greater extent, between one's individual consciousness and the Universal Consciousness. Although how this is achieved by twisting yourself into a pretzel is beyond me.

I don't like the exercise part of yoga, but I do like the relaxation part. In fact, yoga teaches the practice of total relaxation in which no energy is consumed. All these years that I've been lying motionless, I've actually been doing yoga. Who knew?

*AM I CENTERED YET?*

# Garfield's Favorite Yoga Positions...

The Sleeping Locust          The Fallen Tree          The Corpse

## ADVICE

I'm just full of it. To wit: Always be sincere, whether you mean it or not. And always be yourself, unless you can be someone younger . . . and/or richer.

## ARMAGEDDON

Sure signs of the end of the world: Odie joins Mensa; I join Weight Watchers. Naturally, Armageddon will occur on a Monday.

## BALLET

Beautiful but "tutu" boring for my tastes. If only the ballerinas would engage in a little kickboxing . . .

## BASEBALL

Baseball is slow moving, but then so am I. I don't like watching it on TV, but I do enjoy going to the ballpark, as long as I have a good seat— i.e., next to the hot-dog vendor.

## BASKETBALL

I'm like a basketball: orange, round, and frequently stuffed!

## BEACHES

Warm and wonderful! And I don't mean that weepy '80s chick flick. I dig real beaches, as in hot rays and lazy days. Sun, fun, sand, sleep . . . it doesn't get any better than that. I just steer clear of the water. Swimming takes too much energy. And shark bait I ain't!

## BIRDS

Unless I'm eating them, birds are for the birds. That's why my philosophy is, "A bird in the hand would be even better in the mouth."

## BOREDOM

Warning signs that you're getting *really* bored: You braid your eyebrows, then paint little faces on your nails, pretending each finger is a person.

## BOSSES

Most employees think their boss is a jerk . . . and they're right!

## BURPING

I do it loud and proud! Hey, it's cathartic . . . and good gross fun! I once unleashed an epic belch that registered 8.7 on the Richter scale. Now that's what I call a "burpquake"!

## CANADA GEESE

Swooping, pooping, honking nuisances. Why are they still federally protected? And why don't these uninvited guests ever bring any maple syrup with them?

## CARS

I wish Jon would trade in his wussmobile for a fully loaded pimp chariot.

## CHECKING ACCOUNTS

Remember: You're not overdrawn . . . you're "underdeposited"!

## COMMITMENT

I'm not afraid of commitment, provided things don't get too serious. I could commit to spending the rest of my life in front of the TV with a bucket of chicken and a six-pack of slave dogs.

## COPING

When life gives you lemons, shove them up its nose!

## CRUISES

I love these floating smorgasbords! Midnight buffet, anyone?

## DENTISTS

Eating garlic and onions before your appointment will keep drill-happy dentists from dawdling in your mouth.

## DONALD TRUMP
I'd like to fire *him*. And fix his hair, too.

## DREAM JOBS
Mine would be food taster and mattress tester.

## HAIRBALLS
Hairballs in the throat came as standard equipment on us cats. And we love to hack 'em and share 'em! In fact, I've given hairballs as Christmas presents to both Jon and our neighbor Mrs. Feeny. Don't worry—they were gift-wrapped!

## HIGH COLONICS
This new-age "hydrotherapy" is supposed to cleanse your colon and purify your system. Whatever. I think people who pay big bucks to have this done need to irrigate their brains.

## HOME REPAIRS
I'm not what you would call "handy" around the house. But with the proper tools, I can break anything.

## JIM DAVIS
Jim's my creator, but let's face it, I'm the godlike one around here. Jim *is* smart, though—smart enough to stay in the background and let me strut my stellar stuff!

## LACKEYS
"Toadies," "minions" . . . whatever the servile name, you can't be a honcho without 'em. Without lackeys, Julius Caesar would have been just another guy in a sheet.

# GARFIELD
## ON
# EVERYTHING ELSE

## LIFE
Life is a food chain: Far better to be the diner than the dinner.

## MAILMEN
Neither snow nor rain . . . will stop me from mauling the mailmen during their appointed rounds.

## MESSINESS
Wherever I throw it, that's where it belongs. Besides, you call it a mess; I call it my own personal ecosystem.

## MULLETS
Achy-breaky-big-mistakey men's hairstyle. Found in finer honky-tonks and hockey arenas everywhere. If Jon grows one of these beaver's tails, I'm getting out the hedge clippers!

## OPERA
The word may be Latin for "works," but to me it means "ear pain." I prefer my operas to be of the soap variety, and my sopranos to be of the mafia type.

## PIG LATIN
It may not be one of the romance languages, but it's perfect for put-downs. Don't think so? Then ite-bay ee-may!

## PIRATES
Yo ho ho . . . pirates are something you never outgrow! Me favorites are Blackbeard, Captain Hook, and Roberto Clemente.

## PRACTICAL JOKES

I love 'em—as long as they're not played on me. Naturally, I've done the standard stuff: greasing Jon's shoe bottoms, putting water balloons in his pants, shaving his head while he's sleeping. But master prankster that I am, I've also pulled some doozies: varnishing Mrs. Feeny's Chihuahua, duct-taping Odie to a satellite dish, and tying Jon's shoestrings to a jet ready for takeoff!

## PROCRASTINATION

I'll give you my opinion on that tomorrow.

## SAINT PATRICK'S DAY

I like this holiday: It's good green fun! I was born to party o' hearty and sling the blarney!

## SHEDDING

I shed so much, Jon is ready to tear out *his* hair. He's had cat hair on his food, his face, his clothes, his furniture . . . In fact, he once inhaled so many cat hairs *he* hacked up a hairball!

## SHOPPING

No problem is so big it can't be shopped away. But remember, money isn't everything. There's also plastic!

## SNOOPY

In dog years, shouldn't he be dead?

## SNORKELING

Marine life is beautiful, interesting, and above all, tasty!

# GARFIELD
## ON
# EVERYTHING ELSE

## SOAP OPERAS
I love soap operas: love, tears . . . and no fat tenors!

## STRESS
See WORK, MONDAYS, and MARRIAGE.

## SWEEPSTAKES
If you're reading this, YOU MAY ALREADY BE A WINNER!

## USED-CAR SALESMEN
These slimy weasels rank right down there with politicians and spammers. They'll put you in a nice "pre-owned vehicle" faster than you can say "rolled-back odometer." Trust me.

## VAMPIRES
Cold, soulless bloodsuckers that drain the life out of you. See LAWYERS.

## WEATHER
My forecast calls for mostly lazy, with scattered naps.

## WEEKENDS
They should start on Wednesday. That's right: If I were emperor, we'd have a two-day workweek with a five-day weekend. (And why *aren't* I emperor anyway?)

## WINTER
Winter leaves me cold. The only good thing about it is Christmas. Oh, and that dogs don't stink as much.

## ZITS
It's a time-honored tradition that Jon gets a huge pimple right before he has a date. But it's not a huge problem because he only has a date once a year.

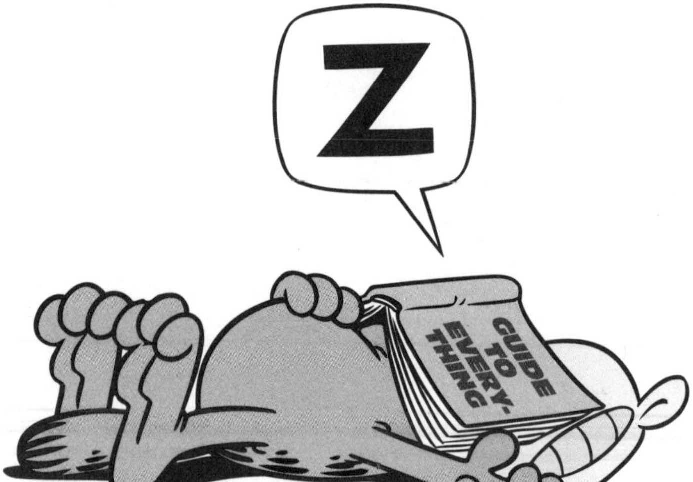
Z
GUIDE TO EVERY-THING